TITANIC

TITANIC

LEO MARRIOTT

SMITHMARK

This edition published in 1997 by
SMITHMARK Publishers Inc.
16 East 32nd Street,
New York, New York 10016

Produced by The Promotional Reprint
Book Company Limited
Kiln House, 210 New Kings Road,
London SW6 4NZ

ISBN 0 7651 0647 7

Printed and bound in China

10 9 8 7 6 5 4 3 2 1

Illustrations

The Author and Publisher would like to acknowledge gratefully the work of Steve Rigby and Geoff Whitfield of the British *Titanic* Society who compiled and captioned the photographs and documents in this book.

Much of this material is of the *Olympic*, the *Titanic*'s sister ship, because of the paucity of photographs taken of the *Titanic* herself.

The copyright holders of the illustrations are credited below:

BFI Stills, Posters and Designs: 97, 98, 100, 101 (T), 103, 104 (both), 109, 110, 111, 112, 113, 117, 151

Christopher Allsop: 60

Electricite de France: 159(T)

Fr Browne S. J. Collection, Irish Picture Library: 40 (T), 56/7, 65 (T), 66, 67, 72, 73 (both), 74, 75, 76 (both), 77 (both), 78 (all), 79 (both), 80, 101 (B), 106 (B)

Geoff Whitfield/Steve Rigby Collection: 63, 99, 114/5, 116, 122, 119 (by permission of Ruby Palmer), 127 (B) and 129 (by permission of Peter Crowe), 133 (TL) ((by permission of Edith Evans), 133 (TR) and 135 (by permission of Elizabeth Verfikula), 133 (B) (by permission of Austin Shorney), 141, 142 (both), 146

IMAX Corp: 158 (T)

Low Films International Inc: 138/9, 152/3, 154 (T)

National Maritime Museum, Greenwich: 55 (both), 107, 159 (B)

PRO: 34, 69, 70, 118, 121, 124, 125, 126, 127 (T), 128, 130, 131, 132, 134, 136, 137, 147, 148, 149

RMS Titanic Inc: 154 (B), 155 (all), 156 (all), 158 (M/B)

Stuart Williamson 160

Titanic Heritage: 33, 65 (B)

Ulster Folk and Transport: 64

Ulster Folk and Transport: Harland & Wolff collection: 2, 4/5, 8/9, 11, 12, 13, 14, 15, 16, 17 (all), 18, 19, 20, 21, 22 (botth), 23, 24 (both), 25, 26, 27, 28, 29, 30/1, 36, 37, 38 (all), 39 (both), 40 (B), 41, 42 (both), 43, 44/5, 46, 47, 48 (both), 49 (both), 50 (both), 51 (both), 52 (both), 53 (both), 54 (all)

via British Titanic Soc: 59, 145 (all)

CONTENTS

INTRODUCTION

Number of passengers on the Titanic

FIRST CLASS
708

SECOND CLASS
510

THIRD CLASS
1216

TOTAL NORMAL LOAD
2436

The official records show 1,523 passengers and crew were lost in total – not 1,522 (PRO and enquiry report). There was a possible confusion over one child in first class, who was thought to have survived, but subsequently was found to have perished.

A few years ago a British television company screened a drama series which centred around the household of a rich family in London. Called *Upstairs, Downstairs*, it drew on the events in the life of the upper class family and the members of its domestic household, the serving classes. In one of the closing episodes the lady of the house announces that she is going on a holiday to America and, in a throwaway line, mentions that she will be sailing on a new ship called the *Titanic*! The writers and producers of the series needed no more dialogue to set the imaginations of the viewers racing ahead to the dreadful fate which was about to befall the poor woman. There is no disaster in history which can be so readily conjured up by the mention of a single word as the dramatic loss of the *Titanic* on the night of April 14/15, 1912 which shocked the whole world and marked the end of an era in more ways than one. At the time the *Titanic*, and her sister ship the *Olympic*, were the largest and most luxurious liners ever built, their sheer size giving an overwhelming feeling of safety and security backed by the knowledge that they incorporated the best traditions of British shipbuilding and the latest techniques of design and construction. Unlike today, Britain was the world leader in shipbuilding; the Royal Navy ruled the waves in no uncertain manner, and any ship emerging from a British yard was automatically regarded as the best available. The loss of the *Titanic* on its maiden voyage severely dented this reputation.

On another plane, the *Titanic* — with its accommodation strictly apportioned in three separate classes (First, Second and Third) and its possible 2,436 passengers served in varying degrees by a crew of 892 — was a microcosm of social life ashore at the time where the upper classes were, for the most part, insulated from the sufferings and privations of the poor. When the ship went down, this division was still maintained to a degree as casualties amongst the Third class or Steerage passengers were proportionately twice as great as those of the First class passengers, although all suffered greatly with no fewer than 1,522* people perishing on that night out of a total of 2,208 passengers and crew. The country was swept by tales on incidents associated with the sinking, ranging from scenes of panic and selfishness to tales of heroism and self sacrifice and the oft quoted image of the ship's band playing popular airs as the giant liner slipped slowly beneath the waves. There was controversy, still raging today, over the actions of other ships in the vicinity, notably the small cargo-liner *Californian* which appeared to have witnessed the disaster but whose captain was alleged not to have taken any action to assist the doomed *Titanic*, and also over the conduct of Bruce Ismay, the chairman of the White Star Line who had commissioned the *Titanic* and who was on board for the ill-fated maiden voyage.

The aftermath of the sinking was felt on both sides of the Atlantic where families, rich and poor, mourned for their drowned relatives. Memorial services were held and then the inevitable enquiries began, both in London and New York. Both fell short of blaming the captain or his crew and cited numerous other factors which had contributed. The most telling outcome was the highlighting of the fact that, although the ship complied fully with the regulations of the day, there was only enough lifeboat accommodation to carry a little over a quarter of the 3,500 souls which the ship could accommodate when fully loaded. As a result of the enquiries, the rules governing safety at sea were drastically changed ensuring not only that ships carried enough lifeboats and equipment to provide a refuge for their full complement, but also that standards of construction and design were greatly improved to give much greater safety margins in the event of compartments being holed or damaged. In the decades that followed, the effect of these provisions was probably to save more people than were lost on that dark April night in 1912; although that would have been of little consolation at the time.

The sea, like the air, is a dangerous and powerful medium and time and time again it has shown its disrespect for the best efforts of men. Since the *Titanic* went down there have been numerous other sinkings, many in the fiery crucible of war, but still others caused by the power of the elements or man's arrogant assumption that he had tamed them. In recent years there have been tragedies such as the *Herald of Free Enterprise* off the Belgian coast, the roll-on roll-off ferry *Estonia* in the Baltic Sea and a horrific ferry sinking in the Philippines in 1987 when over 4,000 people were drowned — finally beating the *Titanic's* ignominious record as the worst peacetime maritime disaster. Despite this, the image of the *Titanic* slowly sinking beneath the waves on a starry April night as the band played valiantly on the afterdeck while the fortunate survivors watched from the pathetically small number of lifeboats is written indelibly into the history of this century — provoking instant images whenever the name *Titanic* is mentioned.

So strong was the pull of the name, that the ship was not allowed to rest undisturbed. Through two world wars and for many decades afterwards, the hull of the ship, still a grave to hundreds and carrying the all the cargo and baggage loaded at Southampton, acted as a magnet in the minds of adventurers and entrepreneurs. Almost as soon as the ship sank there were plans to salvage the wreck, spurred on by rumours of gold and other treasure reportedly stowed aboard. However, it took until the mid-1980s to establish the exact position of the wreck, which lay some miles from the position originally calculated at the time of the sinking, and the first underwater photographs were taken. This event threw the *Titanic* back into the headlines and further expeditions were planned, although there was again controversy over whether the ship should be regarded as a burial ground or whether it would be permissible to salvage items for public display. In the event much was recovered in a French-led expedition in 1987, with other items being salvaged in later expeditions. Exhibitions in France and Britain attracted thousands of visitors, proof that the story of the *Titanic* holds as much fascination for today's generations as it did in the past.

The luxury of the *Titanic* and the Atlantic steamers is legendary. This is sister ship *Olympic's* first class dining room.

TITANIC

PREVIOUS PAGE: *Titanic's* launch May 31, 1911; to her left can be seen the third sister ship (*Arlanza*) under construction.

RIGHT: *Olympic's* double bottom during construction.

The dramatic story of the *Titanic* is inextricably bound up with that of its owners, the White Star Line, and with the history of the transatlantic shipping route. For almost 400 years, following the early voyages of discovery, the traffic between Europe and America grew steadily, despite many wars involving the US, Britain, France and Spain. By the early nineteenth century a substantial trade involving both passengers and cargo had built up: all carried by sailing ships which were completely at the mercy of the elements. A typical crossing could easily take a month or more, with any kind of regular timetable being totally impossible. The introduction of steam power radically altered the picture, although it was not until around 1840 that the first purpose-designed steam-powered transatlantic liners were built. The British Cunard Line, founded in 1839, introduced the 1,154grt (Gross Registered Tonnage) *Britannia,* which set off on its maiden transatlantic voyage on July 4, 1840. The ship could carry up 115 passengers and took 12 days and 10 hours for the crossing from Liverpool to Halifax. Its reciprocating machinery drove two large paddle wheels which gave the *Britannia* a speed of 8.5kts although, like most steamships of the period, a full sailing rig was also carried. The introduction of steamships to the north Atlantic route had a similar impact to that produced over a century later when jet airliners replaced the old propeller-driven aircraft — passenger demand increased leading to larger ships with better economics which could offer lower fares, this stimulating even more demand.

The first significant American transatlantic passenger steamship was the *Washington,* built with German financial assistance for the increasingly important link between the two countries, and which entered service in 1847. At 1,640grt, she was larger than the *Britannia* and could carry up to 300 passengers in two classes of accommodation. Although slightly slower than the British ship, she was cheaper to operate and undercut Cunards fares by almost a third. Following the success of this ship, the Germans decided to start their own line, setting the scene for the intense competition and rivalry which was to continue unabated right up to the outbreak of World War I in 1914. It was during these years that the White Star Line was founded at Liverpool by Henry Threlfall Wilson in 1845, his first partner in business being a John Pilkington. Initially the line employed traditional sailing ships and concentrated on the Australian trade, carrying goods and emigrants on the outward voyages and returning with wool, minerals, whale oil and other imports from the new colony on the return leg. In 1857 Pilkington was replaced by a new partner, James Chambers, and six years later the company aquired its first steamship, the 2,033ton *Royal Standard*, although like its contemporaries this vessel also carried sails. In an uncanny portent of things to come, the *Royal Standard* actually suffered a collision with a large iceberg on April 4, 1864 whilst proceeding under sail on the return from her maiden voyage to Melbourne. Despite major damage to the masts, spars and rigging, the hull was undamaged and the steam plant subsequently functioned perfectly, enabling the ship to make Rio de Janiero for repairs. While these dramatic events were taking place at sea, equally dramatic events of a different nature were occurring ashore. Wilson and Chambers had attempted to amalgamate the White Star Line with two other shipping companies but the scheme, and another similar flotation, failed amongst charges of illegal share dealings. The line got into greater difficulties when a second steamship had to be sold off even before it entered service and a short-lived attempt at a transatlantic service also failed. The company was liquidated and its sole remaining assets — consisting of the name, houseflag and the residue of any business goodwill — was sold for the sum of £1,000.

The buyer was Thomas Henry Ismay, a 31-year old shipping entrepreneur with plans to start a transatlantic passenger steamship company of his own. Finance for his scheme was forthcoming from a Liverpool banker, Gustav Schwabe, who gave his support on the condition that the new line would order its new ships from the Belfast shipbuilders Harland and Wolff, of which his nephew, Gustav Wolff, was the junior partner. Thus the train of events which would lead to the commissioning and building of the *Titanic* over 40 years later were set irrevocably in motion. Ismay and a colleague, George Hamilton Fletcher,

TITANIC

Foreground – *Olympic* during construction, alongside *Titanic*'s keel which was laid on March 31, 1909.

negotiated with Harland and Wolff over the design and specification of the vessels to be built. By 1869 orders for up to six vessels had been placed and Ismay formed a new company, the Oceanic Steam Navigation Co Ltd to operate the ships under the name and flag of the White Star Line. The first pair were named *Oceanic* and *Atlantic*, starting the tradition of giving the Line's ships names ending in '-ic', and they introduced several modern features which distinguished them from other liners of the time. Although still carrying some sail, they were much slimmer than previous ships with a length to beam ratio of around ten to one, compared to the more standard eight to one, and had a deep keel to counterbalance the pressures on the sails. Overall length was 420ft, gross registered tonnage of 3,707, and two four-cylinder compound reciprocating steam engines drove them at over 13kts. More importantly they could carry 166 saloon class passengers in great luxury as well as 1,000 in steerage class accommodation which, while lacking the comforts provided for their betters, was a great improvement on anything which had gone before. The design of the superstructure was rationalised into a single long deckhouse which replaced the many and varied structures of other ships, while innovations such as electrical systems and running water in the cabins were extensively incorporated. In many ways the *Oceanic* could be regarded as the first modern liner and she was extensively imitated.

While the *Oceanic* was being fitted out at Belfast, Thomas Ismay reorganised his business empire and with an associate, William Imrie, formed Ismay, Imrie and Co to oversee the running of the Oceanic Steam Navigation Co and the White Star Line. Over the next 20 years the latter company prospered and it became the acknowledged pace setter on the north Atlantic run, while still operating successfully on its original Australian routes. This was despite the fact that a major disaster occurred in 1873 when the *Atlantic*, sister ship to the *Oceanic*, was lost after striking a rock off Halifax, Nova Scotia. The ship had earlier been battered by a storm which had caused coal consumption to be increased to the extent that her master, Captain James Williams, became concerned about his ability to reach New York and altered course to call at Halifax. Due to a major navigational error, the ship was well west of her calculated position and ran aground on rocks near the shore, only 15 miles from her destination. No fewer than 546 people, many of them children, died in this hor-

rific occurrence which, at the time, was the worst marine accident on record. At the subsequent court of enquiry, one of the incidental causes of the accident was attributed to the fact that ship did not carry enough coal safely to complete her voyage in circumstances which could reasonably have been foreseen, although the White Star Line vehemently disputed this finding.

Over the years that followed, the White Star Line's safety record was such as to cause concern, even by the standards of the time when accidental shipping losses were at a much greater level than today. The 6,594ton *Naronic*, then the world's largest Livestock carrier, disappeared without trace on a north Atlantic crossing in 1893; while the liner *Germanic* capsized in New York harbour in 1899 because of the weight of ice on her upperworks (the ship was subsequently salvaged and put back into service). In 1907 the *Suevic* ran aground near Land's End, Cornwall, when nearing the end of a voyage from Australia and lost over 200ft off the forward section of the hull before being towed off and repaired. In 1909 the liner *Republic* sank after a collision with the liner *Florida* although almost all the passengers and crew were saved due to one of the earliest recorded instances of a radio distress call being successfully transmitted.

Nevertheless, the White Star Line pressed on with its premier north Atlantic services and in 1899 introduced a new liner, regarded by many as the pinnacle of nineteenth century shipbuilding achievement and certainly one of the most graceful ships ever built. This was the *Oceanic* (the second ship of the name) which, with a length of 704ft and a 17,274 gross tonnage, was the largest liner of her day and was also the first to exceed the length of Brunel's gigantic but ill-fated *Great Eastern*, built for the Cunard Line in 1859. By this time steamships no longer carried auxiliary sails and the *Oceanic*'s long hull with its sweeping curves and rounded cruiser stern was dominated by two tall, widely-spaced and well-proportioned funnels, which gave the ship a unique and pleasing appearance. Internally the ship lived up to its external promise with accommodation for 410 first class, 300 second and 1,000 third class passengers, The former were carried in luxurious surroundings including a 400-seater restaurant capped by a 21ft square atrium dome with additional light coming from oversize portholes on either side, while the library was held to be the finest

TITANIC

of its kind aboard any ship. The *Oceanic* was also a fast ship and made many crossings at average speeds in excess of 20kts, although she was never fast enough to gain the coveted Blue Riband. Instead she was responsible for the start of the White Star Line's traditional policy of excelling in comfort, luxury and standard of service rather than competing in the realms of sheer speed. This much-loved ship remained in service right up to the outbreak of war in 1914, although by then overshadowed by much larger ships, and then met an unfortunate end in September of that year when she ran aground off the Shetlands while under naval command.

While the *Oceanic* was doing much to restore the White Star Line's good name, the company underwent a significant change of ownership when it was purchased in 1902 by the International Mercantile Marine Co (IMM) for the sum of £10 million. IMM was a massive shipping conglomorate constructed by its owner J.Pierpont Morgan, an American tycoon who had singlehandedly built up his business to become the largest private banking house in America, before diversifying into railways, steelmaking and shipping. The rich and powerful Morgan dreamed of building up a monopoly of the lucrative transatlantic passenger business and began in 1893 by buying the Liverpool-based Inman Line to add to his own International Navigation Co of New Jersey, which already owned the American Line and the Belgian Red Star Line. In 1902, Morgan restyled his shipping empire as the International Mercantile Marine Co and went on to take over other concerns including the British-owned Atlantic Transport, Dominion and Leyland lines. But the jewel in his crown, and the acquisition which made his dreams a reality, was the purchase of the White Star Line. At the time of the takeover, the line was controlled by Joseph Bruce Ismay, the son of Thomas Ismay, who acted in partnership with his younger brother, James, and William Imrie. Although the Ismay family resisted the takeover, the shareholders had other ideas and were unable to resist the generous offer made by Morgan, to whom money was no object. Faced with a fait accompli, Bruce Ismay co-operated with Morgan and not only remained as chief executive of the White Star Line but, in 1904, was appointed as presi-

Some of the thousands of men employed by Harland and Wolff returning home down Queen's Road, Belfast. In the distance, *Titanic*'s bow is visible.

dent of the IMM group, a post which he held until his resignation in October 1912 following the sinking of the *Titanic*. Although the White Star Line was now totally American-owned, its ships still flew the British Red Ensign continuing to be manned exclusively by British officers and crews – to all external appearances it was still a British shipping line.

While these complex business transactions were being planned and executed, the transatlantic passenger trade was booming as the United States sought to increase its population, and its strength as a nation, by offering unrestricted freedom of immigration to the citizens of all nations. The call was answered by the citizens of almost all European countries, many of which were racked by war, civil strife, religious persecution, or sheer poverty. In their hundreds of thousands they were attracted by the promise of a life of freedom in a vast new country where individual labour and enterprise could bring untold rewards, while the continuing tales, some greatly exaggerated, of fortunes made from sensational strikes of gold, silver and other minerals also fed the demand for a passage to the bold new world. By the turn of the century the major seafaring nations strove to grab the lion's share of this lucrative market and the main contenders were the mercantile fleets of Britain and Germany, echoing the massive naval armaments' race which was also in progress at the time and which led eventually to war in 1914. The main German operators were North German Lloyd (originally partners in the *Washington*) and the Hamburg America Line. In 1897, North German launched the world's largest liner to date. This was the four-funnelled 14,300ton *Kaiser Wilhelm der Grosse,* which was 655ft long and soon proved that she was also the world's fastest liner by capturing the prestigious Blue Riband from the Cunard-owned *Lucania* in the September of that year at an average speed of 22.35kts. This was a major blow to British pride, which suffered a further dent when Hamburg America's 16,500ton *Deutschland* became the next holder of the Blue Riband. Other German liners of the period were the 14,900ton *Kronprinz Wilhelm* and the 19,300ton *Kaiser Wilhelm II*, both owned by the North German Line and the latter ship becoming the third German holder of the Blue Riband in 1906 following its introduction to service in 1903. Fourth

The design of the *Britannic* watertight inner shell proved to be a mistake and contributed to her disastrous end. Retrospectively, *Olympic*'s was extended to above the waterline *(as shown above)*.

TITANIC

ship in this series of world-beating German liners was the 19,300ton, 707ft, *Kronprinzessin Cecilie*, which commissioned in 1907 and could carry up to 1,808 passengers as well as 602 crew. (As a sideline to the *Titanic* story, it is interesting to recall that the *Kronprinzessin Cecilie* was at sea when war broke out in August 1914. Unable to reach Germany, she repainted her funnels in the White Star Line colours of buff yellow and black, and returned to the then neutral United States where she was initially mistaken for the *Titanic's* sister ship *Olympic* when she anchored in Bar Harbour, Maine on August 4. The ship was interned and later taken over by the US Navy before being laid up for many years and finally scrapped in 1940.) By 1914 the German marine was well established and the Hamburg American Line was the largest ship-owning company in the world, its fleet including the *Imperator* and *Vaterland*, two 50,000ton monsters which offered unparalleled luxury.

So what was going on in Britain while all this was happening., As usual (nothing ever seems to change!) the British government was slow to wake up to the fact that its merchant marine fleet, the very lifeblood of the country and its enormous empire, was either being outbuilt by the Germans or taken over by the Americans. It was Morgan's purchase of the White Star Line which finally galvanised the politicians into action and Parliament quickly approved a bill which gave the Cunard Line subsidies to build two liners which would restore British prestige. In return the line undertook to remain British-owned and the ships incorporated features which would allow then to be used as troopships or armed merchant cruisers in time of war. The result of this deal was two ships which, for different reasons, became household names. The first was the ill-fated *Lusitania*, the subject of a notorious demise, when she was sunk without warning by a German U-boat in May 1915. However, her early career was much more pleasing and she quickly rewarded her owners and builders when she regained the Blue Riband for Britain with an average speed of 23.61kts on her second westward voyage in late 1907. With a length of 787ft and a gross tonnage of 31,550, she was easily the world's largest liner as well as being the fastest. Her handsome slim lines were complemented by four evenly-spaced raked funnels which gave an air of speed even when at anchor. As the crew became familiar with the operation of her advanced machinery — new steam turbines geared to quadruple screws — the ship's performance steadily improved to the extent that average speeds on the transatlantic run rose to over 26kts.

Although the Germans and Americans had no answer to this sort of performance, the second ship of the British pair eventually proved to have the edge in terms of sheer performance. This was the *Mauretania* which, by a very small margin, was longer and heavier

Olympic's 15½ton anchor being taken to the ship.

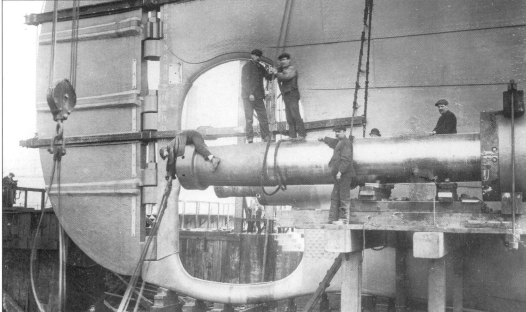

LEFT: *Olympic*'s port and centre propellers.

BELOW LEFT: *Olympic*'s propellers and rudder during outfitting.

BOTTOM LEFT: *Titanic*'s starboard tail shaft being fitted just prior to her launch.

than her sister and on her maiden eastbound voyage showed that she was also slightly faster, making the crossing at an average of 23.69kts. From then until 1914, the two great Cunarders engaged in friendly rivalry until the *Mauretania* set an average of 26.6kts in September 1909, a record which was not broken until 1929 by the new German liner, the *Bremen* — but that is another story. Although built for speed, the two Cunard ships did not stint on the luxury stakes and could carry 560 first, 475 second and 1,300 third class passengers at fares ranging from over £200 in first to around £20 in steerage — these figures comparing in real terms with the sort of money which today's travellers might pay for a crossing by supersonic Concorde or by the cheapest economy air fare respectively.

While the *Lusitania* and *Mauretania* were set to dominate the British-based transatlantic market in the years up to the First World War, J. Pierpont Morgan was determined that his White Star Line would not be outdone. Most accounts credit William Pirrie, the thrusting chairman of the Belfast shipbuilders Harland & Wolff, with the original plan to build two (later three) new 45,000ton luxury liners for White Star. At a dinner held at his Belgrave Square mansion in 1907, he quickly convinced Bruce Ismay of the merits of these ships, which would not attempt to beat Cunard in the speed stakes, but would excel in every other way, particularly in sheer size and in the standard of accommodation and facilities offered. With Ismay's approval, Pirrie went ahead with detailed design work, directly supervising the work of the Harland & Wolff draughtsmen who worked under their Managing Director, Thomas Andrews, Pirrie's nephew, and the yard's chief designer, Alexander Carlisle. The result of their labours showed a ship with an overall length of 882ft, a beam of 92ft and a gross tonnage of just over 45,000 tons. Despite her great size the ship had a slender appearance and carried the almost de rigeur four funnels, although in fact only three were required by the ship's steam boilers, the fourth being added for appearance: it actually contained ventilation ducts. The selection of the propulsion machinery was the result of careful investigation and trials in other ships. The *Lusitania* and

Two of *Titanic*'s engines nearing completion.

Mauretania derived their record breaking performance from the use of quadruple screws powered by steam turbines and it might have been expected that Harland & Wolff would follow suit in their new design. However, as speed was not the prime consideration, the designers eventually came up with a compromise which they hoped would give great economy of operation (always a prime consideration with the White Star Line) while providing sufficient power to enable the ship to maintain a speed of over 22kts which allowed a regular six-day Atlantic crossing to be scheduled in service. The original planned machinery installation consisted of two conventional 15,000hp four-cylinder triple-expansion reciprocating engines each driving 23ft 6in diameter three-bladed propellers. However, the design was subsequently altered to utilise the exhaust steam from these engines which, instead of being vented wastefully up the funnels, was recycled and fed to a Parsons low pressure turbine which was mounted on the ship's centreline and drove a separate 16ft 6in diameter four-bladed propeller. This arrangement was first tested on the White Star liner *Laurentic*, completed in 1909, and showed an outstanding increase in economy and efficiency when compared to the otherwise identical but conventionally powered *Meganatic* built at the same time.

By July 1908 the preliminary design work had progressed enough for Harland & Wolff to make a formal proposal to the directors of the Oceanic Steam Navigation Co (White Star's nominal owners), who visited Belfast at the end of that month. They liked what they saw and a formal letter of understanding was exchanged between the two parties. Indeed, such was the level of understanding between the builders and their customers that no formal contract was ever drawn up, the ships being built on a "cost plus" basis which had pertained to all previous orders. So, on April 30, 1907, Harland & Wolff was authorised to begin construction of two new ships, the first to be named *Olympic* and the second to be the *Titanic*. Subsequently, in 1911, a third ship was also ordered and although the name *Gigantic* was thought to have been chosen, this was changed in the light of the

Olympic's massive boilers await installation.

TITANIC

sinking of its sister ship to a more decorous sounding *Britannic*. Despite the great optimism with which these three ships were planned, two of them had extremely short careers and met tragic ends quite unbecoming of such fine vessels. Apart from the *Titanic*, whose story is told in this book, the *Britannic*'s life was also woefully shortened. Launched on 26 February 1914, she was not completed until 8 December 1915 by which time the First World War was raging. She was immediately commissioned as a hospital ship and made six voyages to the Mediterranean where she was sunk in the Aegean Sea on November 21, 1916, after striking a mine. Mortally damaged, she sank within an hour although, mercifully, only 21 people died, and the many survivors included a handful who had already undergone a similar experience aboard the *Titanic* four years earlier.

On the other hand the *Olympic*, first of the class, had a much longer and more successful career and her story impinges on that of the *Titanic* at several points. The *Olympic* keel was laid down as Number 400 at Harland & Wolff's Belfast shipyard on December 16, 1908, while work on the *Titanic*, Keel Number 401, commenced on the adjacent slipway on March 31, 1909. Work on the two giants progressed rapidly, their massive hulls being straddled by an enormous gantry crane, the largest in the world at that time, which lifted and positioned the thousands of tons of steel plate and girders used in the construction. By the October 1910 the *Olympic* was ready for launching, this ceremony being carried out on 20th of that month, after which the hull was moved into the Thompson outfitting wharf which had been specially built to accommodate the new liners while they were fitted out and completed. At the time of her launch, the ship's hull and main superstrcture was complete and the propelling machinery had been installed. Subsequently the boilers were installed, no fewer than 29 of them in six separate boiler rooms, after which the four tall funnels were erected and the masts stepped. While all this was going on, a host of joiners, carpenters, plumbers, electricians and other skilled craftsmen were preparing and fitting out the accommodation for the crew and passengers. Despite the magnitude of the task, the *Olympic* was completed by May 1911, only seven months after launching, and began two days of formal sea trials on May 29, following which the Board of Trade surveyor issued a certificate of seaworthiness and ship was ready for service. The White Star Line milked the occasion for maximum publicity by arranging for the *Olympic* to sail from Belfast on the same day that the *Titanic* was launched (May 31, 1911) and the double event drew enormous crowds which filled the shoreline around Belfast Lough and jostled aboard the numerous ferries and pleasure craft plying on trips around the harbour.

On completion of the celebrations, the *Olympic* sailed for Liverpool and, after a brief stay, carried on to Southampton where the White Star Line had established its main terminal for transatlantic services since 1907. The ship's maiden voyage was fully booked with travellers eager to sample the world's largest liner and subsequently, under the command of Captain Edward Smith, she settled into a routine that was based around a three-week cycle. It started with a seven-day voyage to New York, which included calls at Cherbourg and Queenstown (Ireland); a three and a half day turnround at New York was followed by the return voyage, which called at Plymouth and Cherbourg before reaching Southampton. A further three and a half days was spent preparing the ship for the next voyage, which started each third Wednesday. This pattern was shared with two other ships, the *Majestic* and *Oceanic*, thus enabling the White Star Line to maintain a weekly return service across the Atlantic. However this timetable was rudely interrupted on Wednesday September 20, 1911, when the *Olympic* set off from Southampton for her fifth revenue-earning voyage, still under the command of Captain Smith. As she made her stately way down the Solent and headed out to pass around the east end of the Isle of Wight, she worked up to a spanking 18kts but was nominally under the direction George Bowyer, a very experienced

Olympic **during her removal to the outfitting dock with** *Titanic* **(in the background) still on the slipway.**

TITANIC

RIGHT: View aft of *Olympic*'s Boat Deck during construction; photo taken on February 7, 1911.

BELOW: Taken on the same day, another view of *Olympic* during outfitting, showing only one funnel in place.

Looking aft at *Olympic*'s Poop Deck during outfitting.

Trinity House Pilot. As she turned to starboard to round the Bramble bank, speed was reduced to 11kts but the wide radius of her turn surprised the commander of HMS *Hawke*, a rather ancient 7,000 ton cruiser, who was unable to take sufficient avoiding action. The two ships collided, the cruiser's steel and concrete bow ram burying itself deep into the starboard quarter of the great liner. Fortunately nobody was killed and both ships remained afloat, the *Olympic* making it back to Southampton on one engine, despite two major watertight compartments being completely flooded. This sorry incident resulted in a celebrated legal argument which decided that the fault lay with the *Olympic* and, although the ship was technically under the control of the pilot, the White Star Line was faced with large legal costs as well as the cost of repairing the ship and the losses resulting from the disruption of services. One apparent source of solace was that the ship had survived a major collision (the *Hawke*, after all, was designed to sink enemy ships by ramming them) and had remained afloat and stable despite serious flooding. This seemed to vindicate the design of the *Olympic* class and helped to lend credence to the myth that they were unsinkable.

After undergoing temporary repairs at Southampton, the *Olympic* returned to her Belfast birthplace, arriving on October 5th and immediately going into the Thompson dry dock from which the still incomplete *Titanic* had been removed. The repairs took just over six weeks and, to save time, the *Titanic*'s starboard propeller shaft and a number of other components were appropriated. Eventually, the *Olympic* returned to the transatlantic run on November 29, 1911 but the work involved in her repairs had a significant effect on the completion of the *Titanic*, although the latter's entry into service was eventually only delayed by some three weeks. The *Olympic*'s career suffered another setback during

RIGHT: *Titanic*'s stern just before launch. This gives a good indication of the height of the ship and the fearsome distance people would be forced to jump as the stern continued to rise prior to *Titanic*'s downward plummet to the seabed.

BELOW: *Titanic*'s bow, just prior to launch.

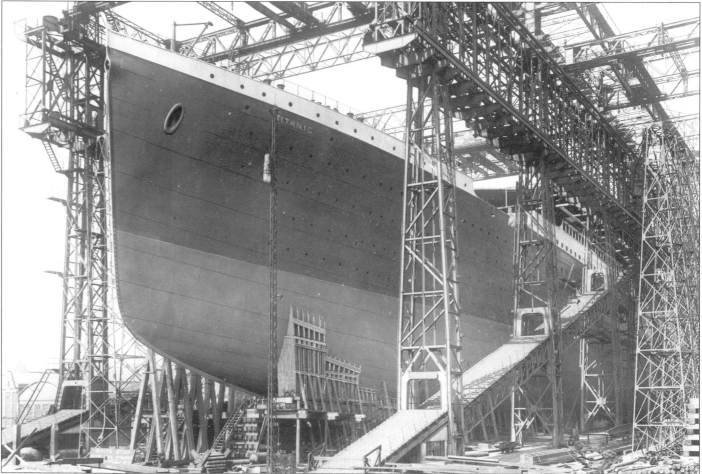

February 1912, when she lost a propeller blade after striking an uncharted obstruction while eastbound over the Grand Banks, some 750 miles off the Newfoundland coast. Once again she returned to Belfast for repairs, spending a week there early in March 1912 and again disrupting work on the *Titanic*. It was during this period that the last photographs of the two ships together were taken. Back in service, she was actually at sea and homeward bound from New York on the fateful April 13, 1912, when she learned of the loss of the *Titanic*, but was too far away to be of any useful assistance. For a couple more years she continued as the flagship of the White Star Line on the Atlantic run until requisitioned for use as a troopship in the First World War. Unlike the *Britannic*, she seemed to have a charmed life and even managed to ram and sink a U-boat. When peace returned, she was refitted and modernised before settling back into the old routine with the White Star Line until her retirement in 1935. Despite her early misfortunes, these subsequent years of arduous service showed the ship was basically sound and able to take all the routine strains and stresses which affect any vessel of this size over a period of some 24 years.

While the *Olympic* was hitting the headlines in 1911, work on the *Titanic* pressed ahead despite the interruptions. As already related and, as might be expected, she was launched amid great publicity on May 31, 1911. The weather was fitting for the occasion with clear skies and sunshine, although a stiff breeze blew up the Lough from the south causing the many flags, pennants and ensigns to stand out and add to the air of excitement. Lord Pirrie, the Harland & Wolff chairman, and his wife acted as hosts to the VIP guests, who included J. Pierpont Morgan and Bruce Ismay, on a specially erected stand near the bows where they witnessed the speeches and the intricate preparations for the launch although there was none of the champagne bottle smashing and other ceremony normally associated with such an occasion. At precisely 12.13pm, the final order was given and the *Titanic*, billed as the largest moving object ever made by man, began her short, 62 sec-

A rare view of *Titanic* during outfitting; note she only has three funnels: the fourth, the dummy, would be added later.

TITANIC

ond journey down the greased slipway into her natural element. Unfortunately the otherwise successful launch was marred by the death of a shipyard worker, James Dobbins, who was fatally injured by a collapsing timber support during the preparations — the unlucky *Titanic* claiming its second life as another worker had been killed during the construction of the hull. Ignorant of this tragedy, the VIPs repaired to the Queen's Island yard where Lord Pirrie entertained his guests with an expansive lunch before they boarded the *Olympic* to return to the UK mainland.

With celebrations completed, work continued on the immense task of fitting out the ship. Originally this was scheduled to have been completed by March 1912, with the all-important maiden commercial voyage advertised as departing from Southampton on the 20th of that month. However, this timetable was disrupted by the *Olympic*'s return to Belfast for repairs that not only meant the *Titanic* had to be moved out of the graving dock but also that men were transferred to her damaged sister in order to carry out the necessary work. A new in-service date of April 10, 1912, was announced and work went ahead at full speed as soon as the *Olympic* sailed again at the end of November 1911. By the following January the *Titanic* was almost externally complete, with all four funnels in place, although there was a considerable amount of internal work to be done. In almost every respect the *Titanic* and the *Olympic* were absolutely identical and consequently there are numerous instances of confusion and mistaken identities. In fact a great proportion of postcards and photographs purporting to show the *Titanic*, particularly those which show the interior of the ship and her cabins, actually illustrate her sister ship. It was only in the latter stages of fitting out that an addition was made to the *Titanic* which served to differentiate the two ships. Following initial experience with the *Olympic*, and at the personal insti-

Titanic **immediately after launch. From here she was moved to the Thompson Wharf for fitting out.**

gation of Bruce Ismay, a steel-framed screen equipped with sliding windows was fitted to the forward half of the promenades on A Deck. These were intended to provide additional shelter from the weather for first class passengers, although the windows were normally bolted shut and could only be opened with a special spanner. It has been speculated that these screens could have impeded access to the lifeboats being lowered from above.

Despite these last minute additions, the ship was ready for her sea trials on April 1, 1912, although these were delayed until the following day due to adverse weather conditions. Tuesday, April 2, was therefore the date on which the ship left her birthplace and moved for the first time under the power of her own engines. At six o'clock in the morning she was moved from her shipyard berth by a fleet of four tugs and, despite the early hour, there were many spectators as the ship was towed out into Belfast Lough and taken downstream to a point off Carrickfergus.

Here the tugs cast off and *Titanic* pulled out into the open waters of the Irish Sea for a busy programme of trials. These included putting to work and testing all her machinery, the steering gear, and making a series of runs at different propeller rpm so that her speed and performance could be related to engineroom indications. One important test measured her ability to stop in an emergency and, with this in mind, the ship was worked up to 20kts at which point the engines were thrown into reverse and full power applied. The resulting stopping distance was around 850 yards, just under half a mile and roughly equivalent to three times the length of the ship — all-in-all a very creditable performance for a 46,328grt ship. After this the *Titanic* set course to the south and ran for two hours in a straight line before reversing course and heading north again for a similar period. These timed runs were completed at an average speed of 18kts. With the ship again at a stand-

Titanic **during fitting out. The alterations to B Deck to accommodate two private promenade suites can be seen. The funnels are still unpainted.**

TITANIC

BELOW: *Titanic's* lifeboats are installed, but as yet her Promenade Deck has not been enclosed.

ABOVE RIGHT: *Titanic* lying completed in Belfast Lough.

BELOW RIGHT: During early March 1912 the *Olympic* returned to Belfast after having lost a propeller blade. *Titanic* was moved from the Thompson Graving Dock so that the necessary repairs could be carried out on her sister ship. This was to be the last time that the two sisters would be seen together.

still, the anchors were lowered and raised, and then she returned back the Belfast Lough where she moored for a few hours while final supplies were taken aboard and non-essential shipyard workers who had accompanied the trials were ferried ashore.

During the day's trials the White Star Line had been represented by one of their directors, Harold Sanderson; Harland & Wolff by Lord Pirrie's nephew, Thomas Andrews, and also by Edward Wilding and a team of nine other specialist known as the guarantee group. As was common practice on such occasions, the latter group would stay aboard the ship at least for the maiden voyage, in order to be on hand to assist with rectifying any faults or problems which might occur. One other important personage who accompanied the initial sea trials, and no idle spectator, was the Board of Trade's representative and surveyor, Francis Carruthers. It was he who, on the return to Belfast at the end of the busy day of trials, signed the *Titanic's* official certificate of seaworthiness which was necessary before the ship was allowed to carry fare-paying passengers. With this accomplished, Harland & Wolff officially handed the ship over to the White Star Line, Sanderson and Andrews conducting the necessary formalities and exchange of documents. After this was completed, and with the crew at their stations, the *Titanic* slipped from her mooring just after 8pm and sailed out into the Irish Sea, leaving Belfast for ever and setting course for her home port of Southampton where she arrived just before midnight on the night of April 3. During the 570-mile voyage further trials and tests had been carried out and at one point the ship had worked up to 23.25kts, the fastest speed she is known ever to have attained. On arrival at Southampton she was met by five tugs, which skilfully turned her in midstream and then manouevred her stern first into Berth 44 at the White Star Dock.

The *Titanic* had arrived!

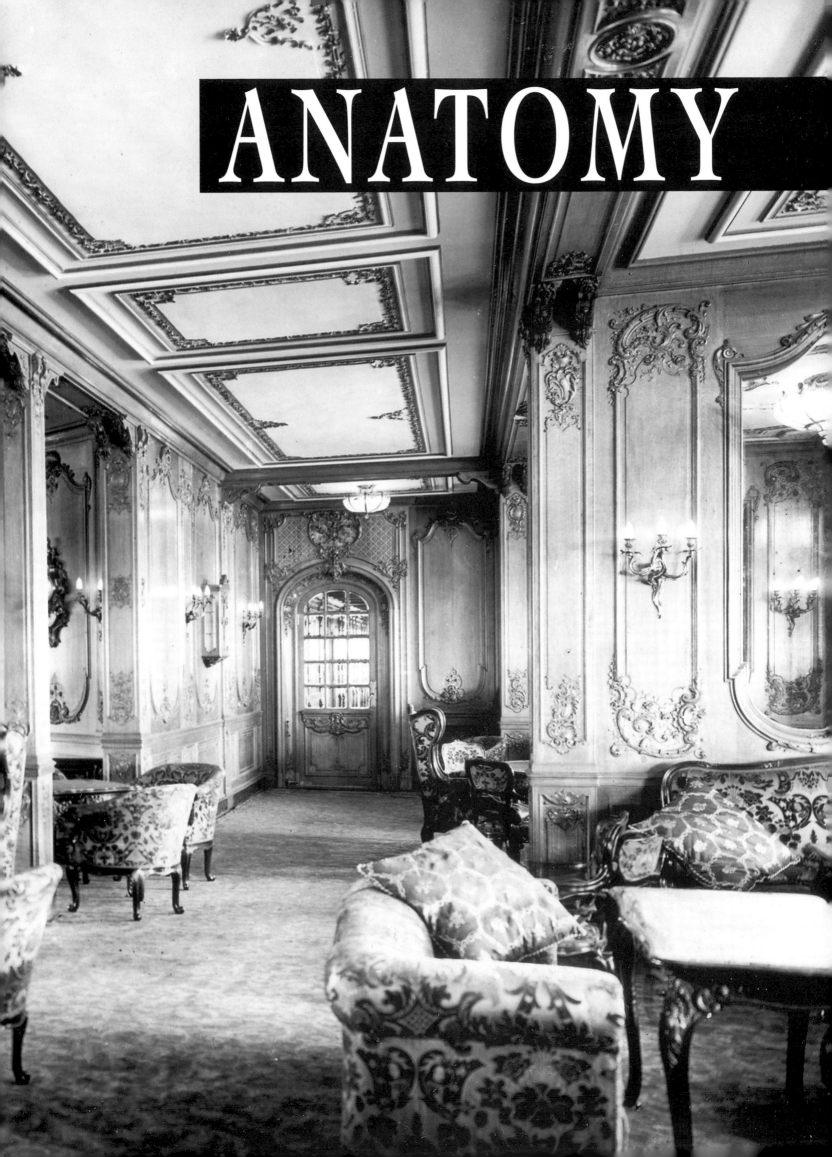

ANATOMY

TITANIC

The sight which greeted the inhabitants of Southampton as dawn broke on April 4 was of a massive but beautiful and graceful ship finished in the White Star Line colours — a black hull with red boot topping at the waterline, white superstructure and upperworks, a yellow/gold band around the hull at main deck level and yellow masts and buff funnels, the latter each capped with a broad black band. The ship's statistics were widely known and quoted thanks to the blanket coverage given to the two new White Star liners in the national, local and technical press of the day. Any schoolboy could probably have recited that the hull had a length of 882ft 9in, a beam of 92ft 6in and a draught of 34ft. Although the gross registered tonnage was given as 46,329, the ship actually displaced some 66,000 tons. Despite the great size of the ship, the *Titanic* was extremely elegant in design, with an almost straight bow, a slightly rising sheerline fore and aft, and a traditional overhanging counter stern. The superstructure decks were continuous and unbroken, while the four funnels were well-proportioned, equally spaced and stylishly raked. Raised forecastle and poop decks left well decks fore and aft, which provided space for the installation of hatches permitting the loading of food and stores. Tall masts were stepped fore and aft carry to signal halyards and also to support the aerials required by the powerful radio equipment which was fitted to the ship — a relatively modern innovation.

For such a large and new ship, the construction of the hull was relatively simple and traditional. A combination of transverse frames and longitudinal girders built up from the keel provided the framework on which the hull's steel plating was riveted. The vertical transverse frames were spaced three feet apart along the whole length of the hull except in the bow and stern areas where the interval was reduced to two feet and 2ft 3in respectively to give increased strength in these vunerable areas. The plates themselves were almost an inch thick and were held in place by literally millions of rivets, which alone accounted for some 1,500 tons of the ship's final displacement. Apart from rounded bilges the hull had an almost square section for most of the midships section, a shape which allowed the maximum usable internal space. The lower edges each carried a 300ft long bilge keel which acted as dampers to reduce rolling, while below the stern were massive castings to support the propellers and the 78ft high, 101ton, rudder. Internally the ship was arranged in eight major deck levels designated from A deck, immediately below the open boat deck, down to G deck, all of which included areas of accommodation for passengers or crew. Below G deck was the Orlop Deck, mainly taken up by the machinery spaces but also providing stowage for cargo and stores fore and aft, and at the very lowest level was the Tank Top which rested on the ship's double bottom and provided the base on which the machinery and boilers were mounted. The double bottom itself was 5ft 3in deep and held water tanks for boiler and non potable (drinking) water.

Of particular interest in view of subsequent events were the provisions incorporated to maintain buoyancy in the event of the hull being pierced and internal flooding occurring. The main safety feature in this respect was the division of the hull into separate zones or compartments by no fewer than 15 transverse watertight bulkheads, each incorporating watertight doors which could be closed by operating a single electric switch on the bridge. In the event of a collision, the main hazard envisaged, the *Titanic* was designed to stay afloat with at least any two compartments completely flooded and would probably float in calm conditions with up to four filled with water. There were no longitudinal watertight bulkheads, a deliberate omission which ensured that the ship would not list unduly if holed. These arrangements seemed justified by the aftermath of the collision between the *Olympic* and the cruiser *Hawke* when, although seriously holed, the former was never in any danger of sinking. Although neither Harland & Wolff nor the White Star Line ever claimed that the *Titanic*, or her sisters, were unsinkable, they were both confident that they would survive all known hazards and that their size, strength and design made them as safe as was humanly possible; neither concern did anything the demolish the popular myth which held that these latest and greatest manifestations of man's creativity and engineering ability were indestructible.

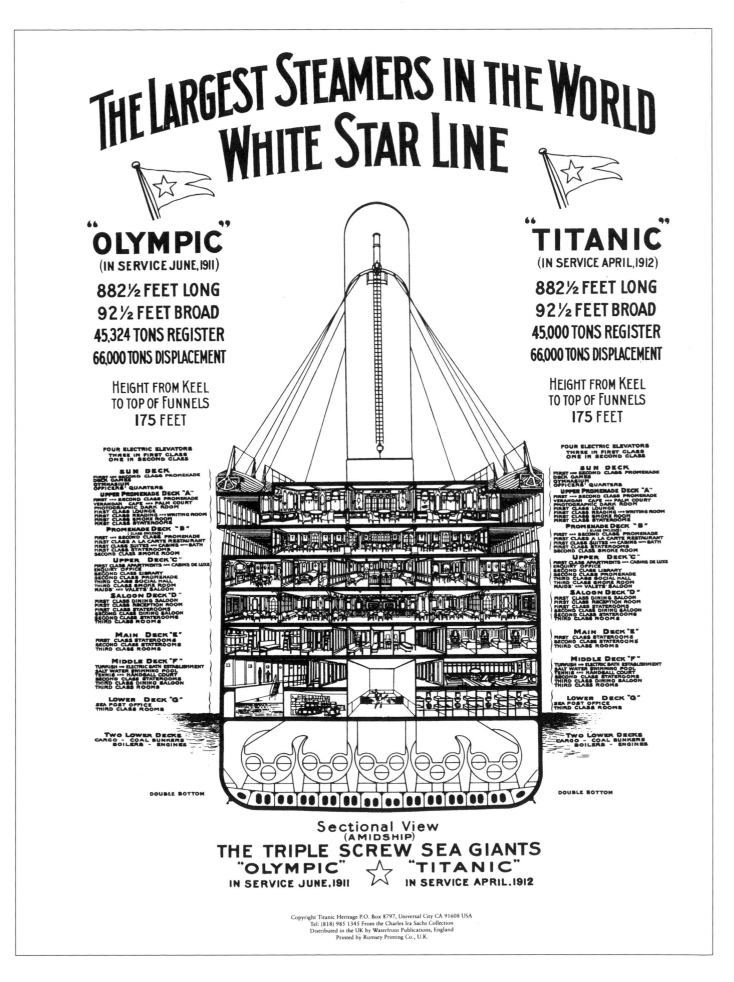

THE LARGEST STEAMERS IN THE WORLD
WHITE STAR LINE

"OLYMPIC"
(IN SERVICE JUNE, 1911)

882½ FEET LONG
92½ FEET BROAD
45,324 TONS REGISTER
66,000 TONS DISPLACEMENT

HEIGHT FROM KEEL
TO TOP OF FUNNELS
175 FEET

"TITANIC"
(IN SERVICE APRIL, 1912)

882½ FEET LONG
92½ FEET BROAD
45,000 TONS REGISTER
66,000 TONS DISPLACEMENT

HEIGHT FROM KEEL
TO TOP OF FUNNELS
175 FEET

FOUR ELECTRIC ELEVATORS
THREE IN FIRST CLASS
ONE IN SECOND CLASS

SUN DECK
FIRST AND SECOND CLASS PROMENADE
DECK GAMES
GYMNASIUM
OFFICERS' QUARTERS

UPPER PROMENADE DECK "A"
FIRST AND SECOND CLASS PROMENADE
VERANDAH CAFE AND PALM COURT
PHOTOGRAPHIC DARK ROOM
FIRST CLASS LOUNGE
FIRST CLASS READING AND WRITING ROOM
FIRST CLASS SMOKE ROOM
FIRST CLASS STATEROOMS

PROMENADE DECK "B"
(GLASS ENCLOSED)
FIRST AND SECOND CLASS PROMENADE
FIRST CLASS A LA CARTE RESTAURANT
FIRST CLASS SUITES AND CABINS WITH BATH
FIRST CLASS STATEROOMS
SECOND CLASS SMOKE ROOM

UPPER DECK "C"
FIRST CLASS APARTMENTS AND CABINS DE LUXE
ENQUIRY OFFICE
SECOND CLASS LIBRARY
SECOND CLASS PROMENADE
THIRD CLASS SOCIAL HALL
THIRD CLASS SMOKE ROOM
MAIDS' AND VALETS' SALOON

SALOON DECK "D"
FIRST CLASS DINING SALOON
FIRST CLASS RECEPTION ROOM
FIRST CLASS STATEROOMS
SECOND CLASS DINING SALOON
SECOND CLASS STATEROOMS
THIRD CLASS ROOMS

MAIN DECK "E"
FIRST CLASS STATEROOMS
SECOND CLASS STATEROOMS
THIRD CLASS ROOMS

MIDDLE DECK "F"
TURKISH AND ELECTRIC BATH ESTABLISHMENT
SALT WATER SWIMMING POOL
TENNIS AND HANDBALL COURT
SECOND CLASS STATEROOMS
THIRD CLASS DINING SALOON
THIRD CLASS ROOMS

LOWER DECK "G"
SEA POST OFFICE
THIRD CLASS ROOMS

TWO LOWER DECKS
CARGO - COAL BUNKERS
BOILERS - ENGINES

DOUBLE BOTTOM

DOUBLE BOTTOM

Sectional View
(AMIDSHIP)
THE TRIPLE SCREW SEA GIANTS
"OLYMPIC" ☆ "TITANIC"
IN SERVICE JUNE, 1911   IN SERVICE APRIL, 1912

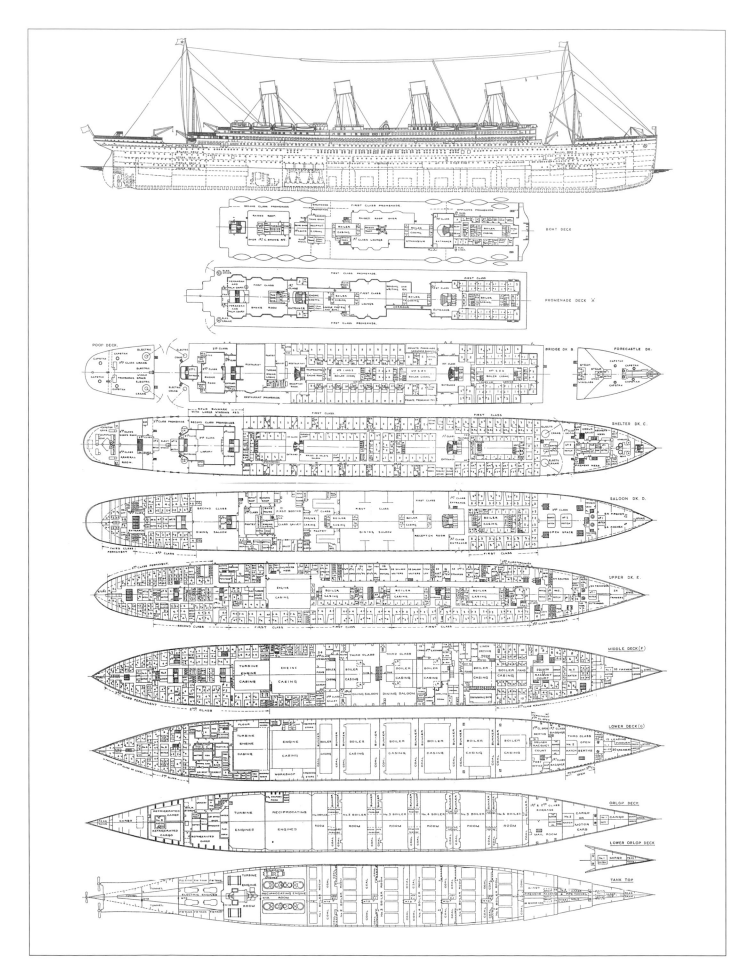

However, what was to prove a fatal flaw in the design of the compartments formed by the watertight bulkheads: they were not, in themselves, independently watertight. There was no covering watertight deck to cap them (as was included in the contemporary Cunard liners, *Lusitania* and *Mauretania*). The effect of this was that, if water actually filled a compartment to above the top of the watertight bulkhead, then it could flow into the adjoining compartment and flood that one in turn. This was one of the factors which contributed to the loss of the ship. At the time of its construction, the designers assumed that this could not happen as all the bulkheads were carried up to levels above the waterline, although seven of them only rose to E Deck level. The remainder of the eight bulkheads extended further to the underside of D Deck. This arrangement provided a freeboard of 2½ft to 3ft to the water margin lines as against the modern requirement of just 3in. This meant eight extended to the underside of D Deck and seven extended to the underside of E Deck. Two of the taller bulkheads were concentrated in the bow to cater for a possible collision, while the lower ones tended to be concentrated amidships, dividing the various boiler and machinery spaces.

At the level of the lower decks, the midships two thirds of the hull was almost entirely devoted to the coal-fired boilers and the steam propulsion machinery. In all there were 29 boilers housed in six boiler rooms which were arranged in pairs grouped directly below each of the three forward funnels. Each boiler room was located between two watertight bulkheads with bunkers carrying up to 8,000 tons of coal lining each side of the bulkhead, while the boilers themselves were arranged laterally across the beam of the ship. Immediately aft of the boilers was the compartment containing the main machinery, two reciprocating compound steam engines, and aft of these was a further compartment in which was installed the Parsons steam turbine. Working upwards, it was not until G Deck (the Lower Deck) level that there was space for any accommodation and even this was limited to crew spaces for stokers and greasers right forward in the bow together with a few third class cabins while right aft were further third class cabins separated from the machinery spaces by the galley stores. The midships section was entirely given over to the boiler and machinery casings and even at Middle or F Deck the boiler uptakes and machinery casings intruded but there was also room for the third class dining saloon, ship's laundry complex, and some crew cabins amidships. Of special interest to passengers were the swimming pool and Turkish baths housed forward on the starboard side, while a squash court, which also occupied part of G Deck, was towards the bow. Otherwise F Deck echoed the arrangement of housing crew and third class passengers forward and a mix of second and third class passenger accommodation aft. F Deck was the first deck to be completely above the waterline and at various points along the ship's side would be found the scuttles covering the coal shutes used for the unpleasant task of coaling ship whilst in harbour.

The Upper or E Deck was the lowest deck in which it was possible to traverse the whole length of the ship at one level and, although pierced by the three boiler uptakes and part of the main engine casing, it contained considerably more accommodation and public spaces than the decks below. Right in the bow were crew spaces housing seaman and coal trimmers as well as a few third class cabins and toilet facilities while the stern section carried more second and third class cabins. Amidships, the entire starboard side of the ship was taken up with sumptuous first class cabins, while the port side housed the hundreds of stewards and waiters who formed a significant proportion of the total crew. A long straight passageway flanking the port side of the boiler uptakes was known as the "Scotland Road" and provided access to the crew accommodation, which also included the engineer's mess further aft. Above E Deck was the Saloon (D) Deck which was the highest continuous deck in the ship and which carried more crew accommodation right forward together with an open public area used by third class passengers. In the after section was the second class dining saloon, which straddled the full width of the ship, as well as more accommodation, mostly second class but including a few third class cabins in the extreme stern. In the area below the fore funnel were some 14 first class cabins, but the rest of the midships section

LEFT: Highly detailed elevation and deck plans for the *Titanic* taken from the original construction plans held by Harland and Wolff. *(8 to D Deck underside, 7 to E Deck underside)*. The design for the ship originated one evening at Devonshire House, the London home of Lord Pirrie, the Chairman of Harland and Wolff. He was entertaining J. Bruce Ismay, the Managing Director of the White Star Line when after dinner they drew up some rough sketches of their ideal ship.

Titanic is most easily distinguished from her sister ship, *Olympic,* by the partial glazing in of the forward third of the promenade deck. This was done after sea trial observations on the latter showed that passengers who wanted to stroll on the promenade deck would do so in greater comfort if they were protected from the elements in bad weather and rough sea conditions.

TITANIC

Titanic lying completed in Belfast Lough.

was taken up with the first class reception areas and dining saloon, both of which stretched right across the ship in the area between the first and third funnels, while in the region below the fourth funnel were the pantries and galleys serving both first and second class dining saloons. The ship's hospital was also located here on the starboard side.

At Shelter (C) Deck level there were breaks fore and aft to allow access to loading hatches which were served by a total of six electric cranes. There was more crew accommodation in the forecastle and under the Poop Deck were the third class General and smoke rooms, these passengers also using the open well deck as their promenade. The rest of the Shelter Deck was given over to first class cabins apart from the second class library and sheltered promenade at the after end of the main superstructure section. Throughout the first class areas of the ship were cabins for the many maids and servant who accompanied their masters and mistresses and they had their own saloon at this deck level. Above them was the Bridge (B) Deck which held yet more first class accommodation, including two opulent suites situated one on either side of the ship abreast the second funnel: these were universally and rightly known as the "millionaires" suites. Towards the after end were more first class restaurants including the informal Café Parisien on the starboard side, while the second class smoke room and open promenade was at the after end. The Promenade or A Deck was given over almost entirely to first class amenities including reading and smoking rooms, a large lounge and the Palm Court areas aft. There were extensive areas of open promenade decks, the forward sections of which were protected by the screens mentioned earlier. At the highest level of the ship was the open Boat Deck with the bridge and officers' accommodation right forward and a gymnasium tucked up against the second funnel. The open areas of deck were used as promenade areas by both first and second class passengers as well as the ship's officers, although some sections were blocked off by the raised roofs over lounge and smoke rooms below.

Mention of the Boat Deck leads to a consideration of the lifeboats carried by the _Titanic_, a matter which raised considerable controversy in the immediate aftermath of the sinking. At the time of the disaster the ship carried a total of 20 lifeboats of which 14 were of a standard design capable of carrying approximately 65 people, two emergency cutters which were permanently swung out and could each carry 40 people, and four collapsible "Engelhardt" lifeboats carrying 47 people. Readers with a mathematical inclination will have worked out that the total capacity of all these came to 1,178, a figure well short of 3,300 passengers and crew which the ship was certificated to carry if fully loaded. Scandalous as this might seem, this meagre provision not only complied with, but actually exceeded, the official Board of Trade requirements at the time. There were basically two reasons for this state of affairs: the first was that, as often happens, government regulations had failed to keep up with the headlong advances in technology so that, by the time that 46,000grt ships like the *Titanic* were being laid down, the rules were based on the 10,000grt ships built almost 20 years before. The second was the whole philosophy behind the new breed of liners which deemed that, even in the worst case, they would take some time to sink, by which time other vessels would be in the vicinity. They would have been summoned by that modern miracle, radio, and the task of the lifeboats would not be to serve as a refuge for those on board but merely to ferry survivors to other ships which had come to the rescue. With this in mind there were more than enough lifebelts (3,560) for all on board but these would be of little use if a survivor had no lifeboat to which he could swim once in the water. The hollow thinking behind this state of affairs was to be sadly exposed on the night of April 14,1912.

However, such considerations were probably far from the thoughts of the passengers who were preparing to board the *Titanic* for its maiden voyage. Instead they would be eagerly anticipating the privilege and thrill of travelling in the world's largest, and supposedly safest, liner and looking forward to sampling the luxurious facilities which had been so widely publicised. In particular, the first class passengers could look forward to a week of comfort and opulence which at least equalled and probably even exceeded anything they were familiar with ashore. Indeed, to these passengers the ship was nothing more than a prestigious five-star floating hotel, complete with all the services and amenities which they would expect from such an establishment. The accommodation which had attracted the most publicity would have been the two millionaire suites on B Deck. Each consisted of two bedrooms with bathroom and dressing facilities between them and a separate sitting

Olympic's **starboard Boat Deck shows four second class lifeboats.**

TITANIC

ABOVE: *Olympic*'s gymnasium windows.

RIGHT: One of the cranes used to stow cargo.

BELOW RIGHT: *Olympic*'s port side Boat Deck looking aft, showing the ship's compass tower on top of raised smoke room roof.

FAR RIGHT, ABOVE: Inside *Olympic*'s bridge looking towards the starboard wing bridge. From this location First Officer Murdoch and Captain Smith saw the iceberg after the collision.

FAR RIGHT, BELOW: View from *Olympic*'s Forecastle Deck looking aft toward the bridge. Note the ship's bell; *Titanic*'s has since been recovered from the wreck site.

These photographs of the first class swimming pool (*Titanic*'s TOP and *Olympic*'s ABOVE) show just how close the sister ships were in layout and construction. They were also the first ocean liners to offer swimming pools to travellers.

room. The larger of the bedrooms was carpeted, oak-panelled and decorated in the French style. It contained a large double and a single bed together with various pieces of furniture including a washstand, dressing table and sofa. The other bedroom was of similar size and content but was decorated in a different style; the sitting room was expansively fitted out and furnished with a large round table, armchairs and occasional chairs, a writing desk, a coffee stool and, rather incongruously, a fireplace and mantlepiece. Each of these two suites had access to a private veranda equipped with chairs, settees and tables and both had a servant cabin and private pantry immediately adjacent. Also on B Deck were 30 parlour suites which consisted of large cabins containing a double bed and a range of other furniture as well as adjacent washrooms and wardrobes. These were furnished in a variety of decorative styles culled from the stately homes of Europe including Louis XV and XVI, Adams and Empire styles.

When boarding the ship, the first class passengers would immediately come into the impressive entrance hall on B Deck, where they would be confronted by the 16ft wide grand staircase which accessed six decks and was over 60ft high, capped at its upper level by a massive glass dome and also lit by a massive 21-light chandelier. For those passengers unable or unwilling to climb the staircase, there were three electric lifts available. Amidships on A Deck was the reading and writing room, a spacious area decorated in the late Georgian style with white panelled walls and moulded ceilings, the central feature being a hooded fireplace surmounted by an electric clock. Lower down, on D Deck and easily accessible from the grand staircase, was the reception room, extending the whole width of the ship and heavily carpeted with the best quality Axminster; on the wall opposite the stairs was a specially commissioned French tapestry. If our passengers were hungry they had a choice of places to eat, ranging from the Grand Dining Saloon, also on D Deck, which could seat 550 and was claimed to be the largest compartment aboard any liner in the world, to the à la Carte restaurant and the Café Parisien on B Deck. The Grand Saloon was expensively decorated in a mock seventeenth century Jacobean style while the à la Carte adopted a more expensive Louis XVI look. Centrally located on the Upper Promenade (A) Deck was the smoking room which was loosely based on English country house of the early Georgian period and, as women were not expected to smoke in those days, it was effectively a gentleman's retreat, rather like the London clubs they would reluctantly have left behind!

For those with a more energetic turn of mind, there was a novel 32ft by 13ft swimming pool which was fully tiled in white and blue. Special periods each day were set aside for female bathers. Even more intriguing was the Turkish and Electric Bath Establishment situated immediately aft of the swimming pool. This was done out in a pastiche of a seventeenth century Arabian style with ornate carvings and original tiling. Hot and temperate sauna rooms were available together with electric Turkish baths and there was a full staff of attendants and masseuses to ease weary limbs. Their customers might well have been using some of the sports facilities on the ship, including the full size squash court, a feature of which the White Star Line publicity placed great store, as it offered a concrete example of how steady and spacious the *Titanic* actually was. A full time professional coach was in attendance and a regular programme of competitions would have been arranged on each voyage. Finally, on the Boat Deck, was the gymnasium, which was provided with the latest gadgets in exercise equipment including rowing and weight lifting machines and, perhaps faintly amusing to modern eyes, mechanical horses where passengers could simulate the pleasures of riding on horseback while skimming across the ocean at over 20kts.

If the first class passengers were well looked after, those in second class would also have had little to complain about. Although smaller, their cabins were reasonably spacious and normally configured to hold two or four sleeping berths. Each also contained large wardrobes and ingenious foldaway washstands, although none had en suite bath or toilet facilities, these being provided in special areas on the centreline of the ship with the cab-

Olympic's **smoke room boasted mahogany panelling with mother of pearl inlay and magnificent stained glass windows.**

FAR LEFT, ABOVE: *Olympic*'s reading and writing room. The huge windows overlooked the promenade deck.

FAR LEFT, BELOW and ABOVE: *Olympic*'s first class Palm Court overlooked the Promenade Deck aft. This room led into the first class smoke room.

LEFT: *Olympic*'s first class staircase showing the clock featuring Honour and Glory crowning Time. Part of the beautiful glass-domed roof can be seen.

TITANIC

PREVIOUS PAGE: Another view of the *Olympic's* first class reading and writing room.

BELOW: *Olympic's* second class smoke room. *Olympic* and *Titanic's* second class accommodation rivalled that of first class on most other ships.

ins mostly grouped along the ship's sides in the after section of the hull. The second class dining saloon on D Deck was oak-panelled but was smaller than the first class equivalent, seating only 394 people. Although more simply decorated and furnished, the second class public areas such as the smoking room, library, and entrance lobby were spacious and roomy and the passengers would certainly have felt that had received good value for the money they had paid.

The lot of the third class or steerage passengers was often thought of as arduous, cramped and uncomfortable. While this might have been true on many earlier ships, the builders of the *Titanic* had attempted to provide a much improved style of accommodation in this area. The vast majority of such passengers were emigrants from Europe, intent on starting a new life in America and, in such circumstances, the voyage across the Atlantic was literally a once in a lifetime experience, which the White Star Line did its best to make as pleasant as possible. The public areas were open and spacious, although the decor was simple and straightforward, generally white-painted pine-panelled or plain bulkheads with wooden furniture. Despite this the meals were still served by stewards and waiters and there was plenty of food available. A typical day's menu lists porridge, fish, eggs, tripe and onions(!), bread, butter, marmalade, tea and coffee for breakfast; soup, rabbit, bacon, beans, potatoes, biscuits, bread, semolina and apples for lunch; and brawn beef, cheese, pickles, bread, butter, jam, tea and buns at teatime. Accommodation was mostly in twin-berth cabins with basic wash facilities. The bunks folded away to give more space in the day and electric lighting was provided. Although rather spartan, they were not uncomfortable and the design was well thought out. The provision of twin-berth cabins for this class of pas-

senger was very unusual at this time, many other ships sleeping steerage passengers in four or eight-berth cabins, or even in communal dormitories.

At the time of her loss, the *Titanic* was manned by a crew of 892, the majority of which were accommodated on E Deck, although 108 firemen were berthed right forward under the forecastle and another 140, including more firemen and the third class stewards, were down on F and G decks. The crew's accommodation and messing arrangements were completely segregated from the passengers and they had their own passageways and staircases to move through the ship as their duties required. When the ship had set sail from Belfast she had been manned by a crew of approximately 120, enough to handle the ship on her short run to Southampton where the rest of the crew would be signed on. The man appointed to command this floating marvel of the age was the White Star Line's commodore, Captain Edward John Smith who, despite his seniority within the company, did not have an unblemished record. Born in 1850, he went to sea at the age of 13 and joined the White Star Line as a junior officer in 1880, gaining his first command in 1887. Only two years later he was involved in a serious incident when the ship he was command, the *Republic*, ran aground off New York and was embarrassingly stranded for several hours before being refloated. On the same day, three crewmen were killed in a boiler accident. In 1890 he again ran a ship aground near Rio de Janeiro but his career continued and he commanded several troopships during the Boer War, these services resulting in the award of medal and a commission in the Royal Naval Reserve as a commander, a distinction which allowed any merchant ship under his command to fly the Blue Ensign instead of the Red Ensign normally flown by British merchant ships. In 1901 aboard the *Majestic* and

Olympic — the extravagantly panelled and furnished Louis XVI-style sitting room belonging to a first class parlour suite.

TITANIC

ABOVE RIGHT: *Olympic* — a further view of the reading and writing room in first class.

BELOW RIGHT: *Olympic*'s first class reception room was a popular meeting place leading into the dining room.

again, in 1906, aboard the *Baltic*, his ships experienced serious onboard fires; in November 1909 he again ran aground, this time in the White Star Line's flagship *Adriatic* in the Ambrose Channel near New York. When the *Olympic* entered service in 1911, he continued this amazing record by almost crushing a tug while berthing at New York and was in command on both the occasions already described when the *Olympic* was forced to return to Belfast for repairs. Nevertheless the company appeared to have had no hesitation in appointing him to the command of the *Titanic* when it was ready for sea, although some sources indicate that he was due to retire on completion of the return maiden voyage. He handed over the *Olympic* to Captain Herbert James Haddock in order to arrive in Belfast on April 1 to take the new ship to sea for her trials. In mitigation, it must be admitted that Captain Smith was generally well-respected by his fellow professionals and some of the incidents in which he had been involved were not his fault. Nevertheless, he seems to have had more than his fair share of problems and fate had not finished with him yet.

Smith's second-in-command on the *Titanic*'s maiden voyage was Chief Officer Henry Tingle Wilde. Aged 38 he was formerly Chief Officer of the *Olympic* and could reasonably have been expected to have remained aboard that ship in order to assist its new captain on his first voyage. However, for reasons which have never been satisfactorily explained, Wilde was transferred to the *Titanic* at short notice and did not board until the day immediately prior to sailing, April 9. This appointment caused a reshuffle amongst the deck officers already appointed, and probably some resentment as well. The original Chief Officer, William McMaster Murdoch, was demoted to the position of First Officer, and the same happened to Charles Herbert Lightoller, who now became Second Officer instead of his original appointment as First Officer. The previous Second Officer left the ship as a result of these changes, a move for which he must subsequently have been eternally thankful, and the remaining four junior deck officers (Pitman, Boxhall, Lowe, and Moody in order of seniority) consequently remained unchanged. Whatever the reasons for the last-minute appointment of Chief Officer Wilde, the result was that the ship sailed on her maiden voyage commanded by a group of officers who had had little chance to work together and whose duties had been changed almost on the eve of sailing.

Apart from the crew, there were two other men on board who would play a very important part in the events about to unfold. Although wireless equipment had only recently been introduced aboard ships at sea, its usefulness had been dramatically illustrated following the collision between the liners *Republic* (a White Star ship but not the one which Captain Smith had run aground) and *Florida* in 1909. The radio distress message sent out alerted other ships so that there was little loss of life. Consequently all new ships were being equipped with wireless, although many smaller and older ships remained without. The *Titanic* was provided with a set which had a normal range of around 250 miles but this could be boosted by atmospheric conditions to significantly greater distances. Power was provided by a 5kW generator, with a diesel-powered standby generator and batteries available as alternative backups. The radio room was incorporated into the bridge superstructure aft at the base of the fore funnel and was manned by two operators who were not employed by the White Star Line, but by the Marconi International Marine Communication Co. Gugliemo Marconi was not only a brilliant inventor, but an astute businessman who realised the importance of his invention and consequently kept a personal hold on its deployment and use. The two operators were Jack Phillips and his assistant, Harold Bride, these two continually manning the set while at sea on a six hours on, six hours off, shift pattern.

Another group not directly employed by White Star, and who were to earn undying fame in the days to come, joined the ship at Southampton in expectation of a routine job. These were the eight musicians hired from a Liverpool agency whose task would be to entertain the passengers in the various restaurants and saloons. Little did they realise that their final performance would be in the most dramatic circumstances imaginable!

FAR LEFT, ABOVE: *Olympic*'s first class à la carte restaurant; it was panelled in French walnut with gilded detail. On *Titanic*, on Sunday April 14, just prior to the disaster, Captain Smith was being entertained in the restaurant by Mr. and Mrs. Widener.

FAR LEFT, BELOW: *Titanic*'s first class bedroom B57.

LEFT: *Titanic*'s first class bedroom B64.

BELOW: *Titanic*'s first class bedroom B38.

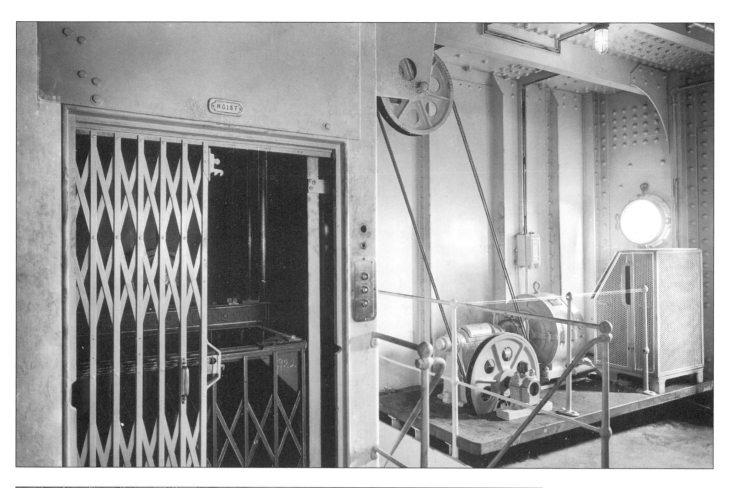

ABOVE: One of *Olympic*'s 10cwt lifts with electric motor.

LEFT: Electrical distribution box concealed behind panelling.

FAR LEFT, ABOVE: *Titanic*'s younger first class passengers ensured that the informal Café Parisien was always popular.

FAR LEFT, BELOW: *Olympic*'s first class dining room.

TITANIC

RIGHT: Main generating set in the engine room.

BELOW LEFT: One of the warren of passageways used by crew members on their way to the deck.

BELOW RIGHT: One of *Olympic*'s washrooms.

FAR RIGHT, ABOVE: *Olympic*'s aft second class staircase.

FAR RIGHT, BELOW: *Olympic*'s third class staircase with the general room on the left and smoke room to the right.

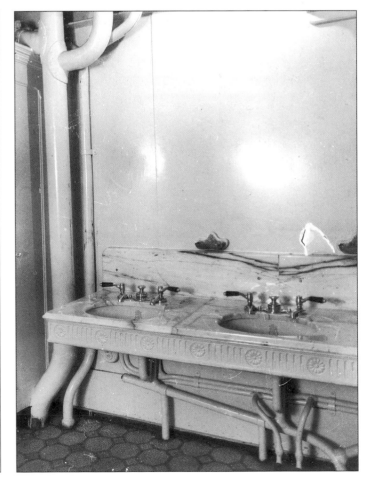

LIFE

TITANIC

At Southampton, Captain Smith's main preoccupation was not with the passengers or crew, but with another problem which threatened to delay or even prevent the *Titanic* from making her maiden voyage at all. The timing of the ship's introduction into service coincided with the final stages of a long coal miner's strike which meant that the fuel was in short supply and Southampton was crowded with other ships lying idle in the port as they waited to replenish their bunkers. The *Titanic* had around 1,880 tons on board when she arrived from Belfast, and picked up more which the *Olympic* had brought across on her previous crossing from the United States. In addition further supplies were taken from other White Star or IMM-owned ships including the *Majestic*, *Oceanic*, *Philidelphia*, *New York* and *St. Louis*. A total of 4,427 tons were gleaned from these sources, but records indicate that some 415 tons were burned while in harbour at Southampton to provide a steam supply to the generators to provide electrical power for various machinery including the cranes, and also for the heating system. Thus when the ship finally sailed she carried 5,892 tons, sufficient for the planned voyage but less than the 8,000 tons she would normally carry. The task of transferring all this coal was tedious and dirty work, the main reason why almost all liners of the time had black hulls, and was not helped by the fact that there was actually a fire in Number 10 bunker on the starboard side of Boiler Room 6. This had started as the ship left Belfast and was not extinguished until the day before the ship sank. Although not quite as alarming as it sounds (bunker fires were common) there is a presumption that this fire eventually damaged the adjacent watertight bulkhead and was one factor which hastened the end of the ship.

With many White Star Line ships laid up because of the coal strike, there was no problem in assembling a full crew and most of those who signed on had their homes in the Southampton area. Filling the ship with passengers was a different matter. Normally a prestigious vessel like the *Titanic* could expect to be filled to overflowing on its maiden voyage but the long running coal strike had disrupted schedules and many would-be travellers had deferred their plans until the situation was resolved. In fact the strike, which had lasted for six weeks, was settled on April 6, but this was too late to have any effect in time for the *Titanic*'s sailing on April 10, by which time only 922 passengers had embarked, although others would join at Cherbourg and Queenstown to bring the final total up to 1,316. This figure was made up of 606 in cabin classes (first and second) and 710 in steerage but was little more than half the 2,436 which the ship could have carried. In the circumstances, it is fortunate that the ship was not fully booked!

Despite being down on numbers, a perusal of the passenger list would have highlighted a fascinating cross-section of travellers. The port side first class suite on B Deck was occupied by Bruce Ismay, the White Star Line chairman, who was accompanied by his secretary and valet. The richest passenger on board was Col John Astor, with his wife, together with an entourage which include a servant, maid and nurse. This party occupied a parlour suite on C Deck, which consisted of a sitting room, two bedrooms, a bath and toilet, and two wardrobe rooms. Isidor Straus, a co-owner of the famous Macy's store in New York, was aboard with his wife, and other well known or rich travellers included Charles Hays, a Canadian railway mogul, Major Archie Butt, chief aide to the President of the United States, Henry Harris, a theatrical impressario and his wife, and a number of American industrialists including John B. Thayer and George D. Widener.

In second class were the eight musicians, who were counted as passengers and not as part of the crew. Other occupants included several families as well as businessmen, teachers, priests, and representatives of many ordinary professions and occupations.

Amongst the third class passengers was a large proportion of Scandinavian families (180 adults and children in total) emigrating to the United States and travelling on the *Titanic* as a result of a concentrated White Star Line marketing campaign in their homeland. Consequently the passenger list included names such as Andersson, Asplund, Hagland, Hansen, Johnsson, Skoog and Svensson. To balance this there were 183 British passengers in steerage, including John and Annie Sage with no fewer than nine children —

the whole family subsequently perishing in the impending disaster, as did the Goodwin family with its six children.

The majority of the second and third class passengers arrived at Southampton just after 9.30am on Wednesday April 10, carried their by the London & South Western Railway boat train which had left London's Waterloo station at 7.30am. A second train arrived at 11.00am bringing the last of the first class and second class passengers. It is easy to imagine the scene as the hundreds of passengers swarmed aboard, confusion ranging as they searched excitedly for their cabins within the unfamiliar confines of the ship, baggage being carried aboard and littering the lobbies, stewards frantically trying to restore some form of order and the general buzz of activity as the ship prepared to sail.

The ship's officers had already spent the previous few days ensuring that everything was ready but, even as the passengers were boarding, the local Board of Trade inspector, Captain Maurice Harvey Clarke, was making his final check that all was well before certifying that the ship was safe to proceed. Despite a rigorous inspection, which included requiring the crew to operate and lower two of the ship's lifeboats, he did not notice, or was not advised of, the bunker fire raging below. While he signed the final documents, the White Star Line marine superintendent at Southampton, Captain Benjamin Steele, received the formal Captain's Report from Captain Smith, stating that the ship was loaded and ready for sea and confirming that the engines and boilers were in good order and that all charts and sailing directions were up to date. As the midday sailing time approached, the officials took their leave and all gangways except one were landed. Already aboard was the pilot, George Bowyer who had been piloting the *Olympic* when she collided with HMS *Hawke*, and his red and white striped flag flew at the masthead. On the stroke of 12 noon, Captain Smith gave the order to sound the ship's horns and the traditional triple blast echoed right across Southampton. As the last gangway was being swung away, six stokers and firemen who had been patronising some of the nearby public houses came running up: it was too late and Sixth Officer Moody allowed the gangway to be landed. The missing mens' places were taken by standby men already embarked for such an eventually. On the bow, Chief Officer Wilde and Second Officer Lightoller confirmed that all was ready, while First Officer Murdoch did likewise at the stern, their reports being passed to the bridge where Captain Smith ordered the lines cast off. As the thick hawsers splashed into the water and the *Titanic* was freed from the land, the same five tugs which had brought her into the dock now gently edged her out into the main channel and turned her bow downstream. The crowd of sightseers and well wishers on the quayside saw the tugs cast off and move clear as the ship's telegraph rang down to start the ship's propellers turning. At first just stemming the incoming tide, the *Titanic* then began to gather way and move down Southampton water, turning to port as she came around the end of the docks complex where two liners were moored, the *Oceanic* alongside the quay with the *New York* berthed on her outboard side. This situation arose due to the number of ships in Southampton as a result of the coal strike and meant that the deep channel which the *Titanic* was obliged to follow was slightly obstructed. By the time that she passed the two moored ships, the *Titanic* was travelling fast enough to generate a suction force (known as the canal effect) on the *New York* to the extent that her after mooring lines parted under the strain and her stern began to drift out into the path of the *Titanic*. Only prompt action by the master of tug *Vulcan*, who managed to get a line aboard the *New York* and steady the swinging stern, prevented a collision, although quick action aboard the *Titanic* also helped as "Full Astern" was ordered and the starboard anchor was lowered to the water-line, ready to act as a brake if required. As the *Titanic* slowed and then reversed, the gap between the two ship was a matter of feet and, once past, the *New York* drifted out into the main channel as tugs fought to control her. Eventually the situation was restored and, with the *New York* now moored in midstream, the *Titanic* was again able to proceed after a delay of nearly an hour — not an auspicious start. However, once under way, things settled down and after disembarking the pilot of the Nab Light Vessel, the *Titanic*

LEFT: **Alfred Samuel Allsop was aged 34 when he died with the *Titanic*.**

TITANIC

turned south and set course for her short run across the English Channel to
Cherbourg.

This part of the voyage was uneventful as both passengers and crew began to settle
into the routine which would occupy their next seven days. Although the port of
Cherbourg had no dock or jetty large enough to accommodate liners, its geographical
position on the northern French coast made it an ideal stopping off point for vessels about
to cross the Atlantic. The White Star Line had commissioned two specially built tenders,
the *Nomadic* and *Traffic*, for the specific purpose of ferrying passengers, baggage, cargo and
mail out to its own ships making weekly calls. The former conveyed first and second class
passengers, while the latter carried the third class passengers and other items. In other
respects the process of embarkation echoed that at Southampton with all the passengers
arriving in a special boat train, the "Train Transatlantique" which was scheduled to leave
Paris at 9.40am and arrived at Cherbourg's Gare Maritime at around 3.45pm. Normally
they would transfer directly to the waiting tenders and be taken immediately to their ship
which should have just anchored after the short crossing from Southampton. On April 10,
these arrangements had been thrown out of gear by the *Titanic's* delay at Southampton and
consequently the 274 passengers had had to wait aboard the tenders or in the railway station until the liner arrived just after 6.00pm.

It was mixed group of travellers who waited patiently for the great ship to appear.
There were 142 first class passengers including Mrs. Charlotte Drake Cardeza and her son,
together with a valet , maid and a veritable mountain of luggage, who were booked into
the grand suite on B Deck, accommodation which had cost them a total of £890 ($4,350).
Another well known party was Sir Cosmo and Lady Duff-Gordon, together with the latter's secretary. In an attempt to remain relatively incognito, the Duff-Gordons had booked
themselves using the surname Morgan, also the surname of the owner of IMM and the
White Star Line, J. Pierpont Morgan. Whether there was any significance in this choice of
alias remains one of the *Titanic's* many coincidences and unsolved mysteries. An extremely rich passenger joining at Cherbourg was Benjamin Guggenheim, a member of dynasty
which had made its money from mining, metal dealing and industrial machinery. Among
the 30 second class passengers was a well-known contemporary marine artist, Samuel Ward
Stanton, and the rather grandly titled Baron Alfred von Drachstedt. The latter made a great
fuss about what he considered to be the poor standard of the second class accommodation
and succeeded in being upgraded to first class after paying part of the fare difference.
Although he subsequently survived the sinking, it transpired at the later inquiry that he was
no "Baron" at all, just plain Mr. Alfred Nournay. The new third class passengers were a
very mixed bunch who came from a wide variety of Balkan and Middle East countries and
had already had an arduous journey across the Mediterranean to Marseilles and then by rail
through France to join the boat train from Paris. For them the delay at Cherbourg must
have seemed interminable and they were, no doubt, heartily relieved to be settled aboard.

The *Titanic* dropped anchor in the roadstead at Cherbourg as the sun was setting just
after 6.30pm. She remained for only an hour and a half, embarking passengers from the
tenders but also dropping off 13 first class and seven second class passengers whose journey
— fortunately for them — terminated at Cherbourg. As the daylight faded, the massive
ship rode quietly at anchor with all her lights blazing, creating an image which was cap-
tured on film and was remembered by local people for many years afterwards. Just before
8.00pm, a triple blast from the horns alerted the town to the fact that the ship was about
to sail and minutes later the anchor was aweigh as the *Titanic* turned under her own power
and edged slowly out of the harbour before gathering speed and setting off westward into
the night. While the passengers dined and then slept through their first night aboard, the
ship rounded Land's End and turned northwest to cross the St.George's Channel before
arriving off Queenstown (currently known as Cobh) on the south coast of Ireland at
11.30am the next day. Here the *Titanic* anchored some two miles offshore and a further
group of passengers was ferried out from the jetty at the Queenstown railway station by

TITANIC

BELOW: April 1912 – *Titanic* birthed at Southampton.

FAR RIGHT, ABOVE: 10 April 1912. Passengers boarding the *Titanic* at Southampton Docks.

FAR RIGHT, BELOW: *Titanic* leaving Southampton for the first and last time.

the tenders *America* and *Ireland*. Of the 120 people who came aboard, all but seven were destined for third class, the others being second class passengers. 1,385 sacks of mail were loaded, while only seven passengers officially disembarked, one of them subsequently proving to be of the utmost interest to researchers and historians looking into the story of the *Titanic*. This was Frances Browne, a teacher and a student priest, whose subsequent value lay in the camera and exposed photographic plates which he took with him (some of which are reproduced here). A keen amateur photographer, Brown had taken an extensive series of photographs of the ship, mostly in the second class areas where he had travelled, and also took several photographs as he disembarked including the last known photograph of the captain, posed looking down from the lofty heights of his bridge (see page 80). A photographer of the local paper, the *Cork Examiner*, also took many photographs at this time and the two collections today form a major and valuable archive relating to the *Titanic* story.

Unbeknown to anybody else aboard the liner, the tenders speeding back to the shore as the anchor was raised included one deserting crewman — a 24-year old stoker named John Coffey. As he gave his home address as Queenstown when he signed on, it is generally thought that he had planned from the start to jump ship at Queenstown as a way of getting a free ride home. If this was the case, then his plan had an even happier outcome than he could have imagined at the time. However, nobody aboard the *Titanic* gave any thought to the missing stoker as the anchor was brought inboard for the last time and the great propellers began to turn yet again after a rest of only two hours. With smoke rising from her funnels as the firemen and trimmers sweated below to stoke up the boilers, the ship's head turned to the west and she gradually worked up to her cruising speed. As the land faded astern, a lone piper struck up on the third class promenade deck aft and played the sentimental air "Erin's Lament". The piper was Eugene Daly, who had entertained his fellow passengers as they had come out in the tender and now played a farewell to the homeland he never expected to see again — although, of course, he had no inkling of what lay ahead and in fact actually survived the sinking.

TITANIC

The *New York*'s stern is drawn towards *Titanic* by the Canal Effect. See page 61.

While the ship lay off Queenstown, the White Star Line chairman, Bruce Ismay, is reported to have had a long discussion with Chief Engineer Joseph Bell. While there were no witnesses to this conversation, Ismay himself subsequently admitted of an intention to run the ship at full speed on the Monday or Tuesday (April 15 or 16) given suitable weather conditions. In fact the weather was remarkably pleasant for the time of the year with only light winds, clear skies and very little swell. Certainly the latter was not enough to worry a ship the size of the *Titanic* and several passengers' accounts of this stage of the voyage attest to the steadiness of the ship. All classes now settled into the routine of the voyage and took advantage of the various facilities on offer, although there was little in the way of formally organised activities such as one might find on a cruise ship today. Most people were quite happy to relax in the saloons and lounges, wiling away the time between the meals which formed the highpoints of the day. Breakfast was available between 8.30 and 10.30am, lunch was served from 1.00 to 2.30pm and dinner between 6.00 and 7.30pm. Mealtimes were signalled by the ship's bugler, P. Fletcher, whose vibrant musical cadences called the passengers to their various dining saloons: 532 seated at once in First class, 394 in Second and 473 in Third. Even with these figures, two sittings would normally have been necessary to allow a full passenger load to dine. However, the fact that the *Titanic* was little more than half full on this voyage meant that all could be accommodated in one go, especially as those first class passengers who did not wish to be tied to set mealtimes could eat in the à la carte restaurant at anytime between 8.00am and 11pm. In fact these passengers could, if they so wished, elect to take all their meals in this establishment and were granted a rebate of $15 or $25 if they exercised this option in recognition of the fact that they would pay separately for any meals taken. First class passengers could also use the swimming pool, Turkish and electric baths, the squash court and the gymnasium in order to work up an appetite or to work off the effects of a meal; tickets for these various establishments were available from the purser's enquiry office on C Deck. For the less energetic, particularly in second and third class where the facilities were less lavish, the traditional shipboard occupations of reading, playing cards, attending concerts and dances and just resting or sleeping were the order of the day.

While the passengers relaxed, the crew busied themselves with the ship's routine. At their head was the grand figure of Captain Smith, who made his rounds of inspection every day at 10.30am, following a daily meeting at 10.00am with the various heads of department. This was ordained by the White Star Line regulations and was meticulously carried out: the captain, dressed in full uniform with medals, made his way through all parts of the ship including public areas of all three classes, the dining rooms and galleys, the bakery, the hospital, workshops and stores until finally he worked his way down to machinery spaces where he was met and escorted by the Chief Engineer. With his inspection of the ship complete, Captain Smith would return to the bridge where he would call the attention of his officers to any points arising from his tour of the ship and would update himself on the ship's progress, poring over the charts and checking the ship's position. He might also have received and read the various radio messages directed to the ship or himself, or checked over general messages broadcast by other vessels within range. In this respect the work of the radio operators, Bride and Philips, was absolutely vital, as wireless communications became essential to the everyday running of the ship rather than an interesting novelty. Many of the messages would be social in nature: various ships which the *Titanic* passed making traditional greetings and offering sentiments of congratulations and good wishes to the stately liner on her maiden voyage.

Titanic **leaves Southampton on her maiden voyage: relatives and friends wave the travellers off.**

TITANIC

RIGHT: The official docu-
ment issued on 12 April
1912 by the Marine
Department of the Board
of Trade showing that the
Titanic was passed fit to
sail. It shows that the
inspectors were fully satisfied that she was in good
order and condition.

Titanic was officially an
'Emigrant Ship'. This was
defined as any ship that
carried more than 50
steerage passengers from a
British port to any port
outside Europe.

The ship was indeed performing well at this point. With the steam from the boilers turning the propellers at 70, later increased to 75, revolutions per minute, the ship sliced through the light seas building up to a steady 21.5kts throughout the Thursday evening and Friday morning, to record a distance run in the 24 hours to noon of 386 miles. In the next 24 hours she logged 519 miles, the greater distance reflecting that the previous day's figure had commenced from a standing start at Queenstown. Speed was increased slightly on Saturday and Sunday as the last of the ship's 24 main boilers was fired up and 546 miles were covered up to noon on April 14 for an average of 22.5kts. During the fateful Sunday, preparations were under way to light up the five auxiliary boilers with the possible inten-tion of a maximum speed run on the Monday. The modest increase in speed and the asso-ciated activity led many passengers to speculate that the *Titanic* was going to make an attempt on the Blue Riband record for an Atlantic crossing, which was held by the *Mauretania*. Such speculation was totally misinformed as there was no way the *Titanic* could match the smaller but much more powerful rival Cunarder, which had notched up over 27kts on its record breaking run in 1907. However, it was entirely possible that Ismay and Smith had decided to take the opportunity offered by the good weather to see if the *Titanic* could beat her sister ship's best speed of 22.75kts whilst in service trim. If any such attempt was to be made, it would have to be of relatively brief duration as there was not enough coal on board to sustain maximum speed for the remainder of the crossing.

As well as recording the speed, Captain Smith and his navigating officers would have regularly checked on the ship's position in order to ensure that she was keeping to her planned course. This followed a standard summer westbound route known as the Outward Southern Track, which had been agreed by all the major shipping companies in 1899 and, from the Fastnet Rock off the south coast of Ireland, followed a great circle route to posi-tion 42°N, 47°W, and thereafter by great circle or rhumb line to the Nantucket Light Vessel. For the purposes of this agreement, summertime was defined as January 15 to August 15. This route was generally far enough south to be clear of any danger of ice, and there had only been three occasions since 1898 when any significant ice had affected ship-ping following the prescribed track. However the winter of 1912 had been exceptionally mild in northern latitudes, causing large ice floes and even whole sheets of pack ice to break away from the Arctic icecap and drift southward towards the shipping lanes. By one of those geophysical quirks which often cause freak conditions, the normally warm Gulf Stream which flows eastward across the Atlantic to northern Europe was sited further south than was normal, a factor which allowed the ice to drift yet further south than would nor-mally be the case and right across the track followed by the *Titanic* and many other ships. Indeed, on the very day that the *Titanic* left Southampton, the French liner *Niagara* report-ed that he was stopped and damaged following a collision with ice at 44°07'N, 50°40'W. This was over 100 miles north of the *Titanic's* planned course but, nevertheless, gave an early warning of possible hazards. As the great ship set off from Queenstown, other reports were being transmitted by at least 20 ships at various times over the period April 11–14. By no means all of these reached the *Titanic* but there is irrefutable evidence that enough were picked up to ensure that Captain Smith was well aware of the potential danger.

The first of these received on the fateful Sunday came from the Cunard-owned *Caronia* (Captain Barr), eastbound from New York, which transmitted a warning by wire-less at 9.00am specifically addressed to the *Titanic*. This read, "Captain, *Titanic* — Westbound steamers report bergs, growlers and field ice in 42 degrees North from 49 degrees to 51 degrees West, April 12. Compliments, Barr." This lay right on the *Titanic's* track and could not have been clearer. A copy was delivered personally to Captain Smith who had it posted on the bridge after noting its contents. A further report, originating from the Greek ship *Athinai*, reported icebergs and large quantities of field ice at 41°51'N, 49°52'W. This message was relayed by the White Star Line ship *Baltic* and was received in the *Titanic's* wireless office at 1.42pm. By this time, the passengers who had been enjoying the spring sunshine on the *Titanic's* promenade decks were beginning to retire to their var-

Surveys 27.

M23780

REPORT OF SURVEY

OF

AN EMIGRANT SHIP

Note.—Cancel the portions of this form that do not apply.

BOARD OF TRADE RECEIVED 11 APR 1912 MARINE SHIP

BOARD OF TRADE, SURVEYORS' OFFICE No. 401 11 APR 1912 QUEENSTOWN

Name and official number.	Port of registry.	Tonnage.		Single, twin, triple or quadruple screw. Registered horse-power.	Where and when built.	in dry-dock.
		Gross.	Net.			
"Titanic" 131.428	Liverpool	46328	21831	Triple Screw	Belfast 1912	Belfast 6-3-12

Date of expiration of passenger certificate.	Mean draught of water and freeboard.	Name and address of owner or agent.	Intended voyage.
2-4-13	34' 0" 31. 4	Oceanic Steam Navigation Co Ltd 30 James Street Liverpool	Foreign

MASTER AND OFFICERS.

Rank.	Name in full.	Number of certificate.	Grade.
Master	Edward John Smith	14102	Ex master
First Mate ...	Wm McMaster Murdoch / Henry Tingle Wilde	025480 027371	Ex Master Ex mast
Second Mate ...	Chas Herbert Lightoller	024706	Ex master
First Engineer	Joseph Bell	19224	1st Class
Second Engineer ...	Wm Edward Farquharson	12883	1st Class

LIFE-SAVING APPLIANCES.

Description of boats and rafts.	No.	Cubic contents in feet.	No. of persons they will accommodate.	Materials.	Number under davits.	Are they so placed as to be readily got into the water?	Are they provided with the equipments required by the rules?
Boats, Section A.	14	9172	910	Wood	14	Yes	Yes
Boats, " B.	✓						
Boats, " C.	✓						
Boats, " D.	2	648	80	Wood	2	Yes	Yes
Boats, " E. Collapsible	4	—	188	Wood with Canvas sides	—	Yes	Yes.

TITANIC

Titanic's Certificate for Clearance as issued by The Board of Trade on April 13, 1912, for an emigrant ship. This gives passenger details broken down by age, sex and marital status. The lower paragraph states:

"I hereby certify that the particulars inserted in the above form are correct. I also certify that all the requirements of the Merchant Shipping Acts relating to emigrant ships, so far as they can be complied with before the departure of the ship, have been complied with, and that the ship is, in my opinion, seaworthy, in safe trim, and in all respects fit for her intended voyage; that she does not carry a greater number of passengers than in the proportion of one statute adult to every five superficial feet of space clear for exercise on deck; and that her passengers and crew are in a fit state to proceed.

Dated at Cherbourg this 10th day of April 1912."

This certificate had to be completed by the Emigration Officer at each port from which the emigrant ship took on passengers.

Surveys 32.

ISSUED BY THE BOARD OF TRADE.

SURVEY OF AN EMIGRANT SHIP.

Certificate for Clearance.

Ship's Name and Official Number. (1.)	Port of Registry, and Tonnage. (2.)		Name of Master. (3.)
Titanic 131428	Gross. 46328	Register. 21831	E. J. Smith

Port of Departure. (4.)	Ports of Call. (5.)	Destination. (6.)
Southampton	Cherbourg Queenstown	New York

CABIN PASSENGERS.

Adults (12 years and upwards).				Children.				Total Cabin Passengers.	Equal to Adults computed by Part III. M. S. Act, 1894.
Married.		Single.		Between 1 and 12		Under 1 Year.			
Male. (7.)	Female. (8.)	Male. (9.)	Female. (10.)	Male. (11.)	Female. (12.)	Male. (13.)	Female. (14.)	(15.)	(16.)
52	52	196	101	10	12	4	·	427	412

STEERAGE PASSENGERS.*

Adults (12 years and upwards).				Children.				Total Steerage Passengers.	Equal to Adults computed by Part III. M. S. Act, 1894.
Married.		Single.		Between 1 and 12.		Under 1 Year.			
Male. (17.)	Female. (18.)	Male. (19.)	Female. (20.)	Male. (21.)	Female. (22.)	Male. (23.)	Female. (24.)	(25.)	(26.)
25	25	315	74	22	28	3	3	495	464

CREW.

Deck Department. (27.)	Engine Department. (28.)	Stewards' Department. (29.)	Total Crew. (30.)	Equal to Adults computed by Part III. M. S. Act, 1894. (31.)
73	325	494	892	892

Total Number actually on board, including Crew

* Total Number of Statute Adults (as Steerage Passengers), exclusive of the Master, Crew, and Cabin Passengers, which the Ship can legally carry according to space allotted	Clear Space in Sq. Ft.	Number of Beds fitted.
1735	26992	1134

I hereby certify that the particulars inserted in the above down are correct. I also certify that all the requirements of the Merchant Shipping Acts relating to emigrant ships, so far as they can be complied with before the departure of the ship, have been complied with, and that the ship is, in my opinion, seaworthy, in safe trim, and in all respects fit for her intended voyage; that she does not carry a greater number of passengers than in the proportion of one statute adult to every five superficial feet of space clear for exercise on deck; and that her passengers and crew are in a fit state to proceed.

this APR 10 1912 day of 19

Dated at Southampton

M. H. Clarke

Emigration Officer, or Assistant Emigration Officer.

(238x) (62245) Wt. 30276/150 3000 12-10 W B & L

ious lounges and cabins as the air temperature was becoming noticeably colder. The *Baltic's* message was taken to the bridge and then passed on to Captain Smith who was lunching with J. Bruce Ismay. After reading it, he passed it on to Ismay, remarking that the ship might soon encounter ice itself. Ismay apparently retained the message for several hours, showing it to several other passengers, before it was finally retrieved and posted on the bridge at around 7.15pm in the evening. Much has been made of the fact that Ismay kept the message, and it has been suggested that he did so deliberately for reasons best known to himself, perhaps fearing that it would prevent the high speed run planned for the following day. Whether such motives were present is really immaterial, as there were many other warnings which were quite sufficient to ensure that both captain and crew were aware of the potential dangers looming ahead that night.

In fact another was received within minutes, this time from the German liner *Amerika* which reported two large icebergs at 41°27'N, 50°8'W. However this was not addressed to the *Titanic* but to the US Navy Office in Washington DC and so the radio operators merely filed it for onward transmission when the ship came in range of the radio station at Cape Race, Newfoundland, later that evening. There is no evidence that it was ever passed on to Captain Smith or any other officer. Another message was picked up at 7.30pm from the Leyland Line ship *Californian* reporting three large icebergs south of her position at 42°3'N, 49°9'W. Again this message was not addressed to the *Titanic* but on this occasion the radio operator on duty, Bride, subsequently stated that he passed it on to an unamed officer. Yet another message came in, addressed to the *Titanic* and other ships, at 9.40pm from a ship named the *Mesaba*, reporting pack ice, icebergs and field ice at in an area bounded by 42°N to 41°25'N and 49° to 50°30'W — totally straddling the spot where the *Titanic* eventually went down. Unfortunately, there is no definite evidence that this message ever reached the bridge, although as it was directly addressed it certainly should have been passed on.

One message which was acknowledged and must have been brought to the attention of the bridge was from a British cargo ship, the SS *Rappahannock*, which reported that she had just passed through a heavy icefield and had observed several icebergs. Although the message did not say so, this ship had actually suffered some damage to her steering from the ice. The interesting point about this exchange, which occurred at 10.30pm, was that it was not transmitted by radio but by visual signal lamp, indicating clearly that the *Titanic* was now very close to the ic field. Less than half an hour later the *Californian* began to transmit a message directly to the *Titanic* stating that she was stopped and completely surrounded by ice, but this message interfered with transmissions to Cape Race from the larger ship, whose operator curtly ordered the *Californian* to stop transmitting.

Earlier in the day, Captain Smith had ordered that planned change of course at 47°W should be delayed for 30 minutes with the result that the ship subsequently ran some 10 miles south of what would have been her original course. His reasons for this order will never be known, although if it was intended to keep the ship clear of the icefields reported ahead, it was not the major alteration which would have been expected in the circumstances. As the evening was drawing on, the temperature was dropping steadily, from 6°C at 7.00pm to 4°C only half an hour later, and only 0.5°C (barely above freezing) at 9.00pm. With the dropping temperature and conscious of the possibility of ice ahead, First Officer Murdoch ordered an iceberg watch to be set with two lookouts in the crow's nest on the foremast. Various officers had made their own estimates of when the reported icefield might be encountered, these varying between 9.30pm and 11.00pm, but by this stage nobody seriously doubted that there was a definate hazard ahead. During the early part of the evening Captain Smith had been dining with a party in the à la carte restaurant but left at 8.50pm and went up to the bridge where he spoke to Second Officer Lightoller, by then officer of the watch. Already Lightoller had noted the dropping temperature and had advised the ship's carpenter, J. Maxwell, and the Chief Engineer that they should respectively check the fresh water and boiler water tanks in the ship's bottom as there was a danger of their contents freezing. When the captain came to the bridge, he was appraised of the situation and the measures so far ordered and during the next 20 minutes the conversation touched on the extremely unusual calm weather being experienced and the difficulties of spotting icebergs in such conditions, particularly as there was no moon that night although the sky was clear and stars could be seen. Despite the topic, no specific mention was made of the warnings already received and at around 9.20pm Captain Smith retired to his sea cabin, immediately abaft the bridge on the starboard side, leaving instructions that he was to be called, saying, "If it becomes at all doubtful, let me know. I will be just inside." Although not specifically stated, Lightoller understood this to mean that he was to be called if ice was sighted, again confirming that everybody was alert for such a possibility.

After the captain had gone, Lightoller passed an order to the lookouts in the crow's nest to keep "a sharp lookout for ice, particularly small ice and growlers" and asked that this reminder be passed on to their reliefs, Frederick Fleet and Reginald Lee, when they took over at 10.00pm. Lightoller himself was relieved by First Officer Murdoch at 9.30pm. The entries in the ship's log at this point show that the ship was making a steady 22.5kts and that the air temperature was right on freezing (0°C). Whatever precautions had been considered necessary in view of the approaching ic field, a reduction in speed was obviously not given serious consideration. As the ship sped on through the still night, the sea temperature dropped even further to half a degree below freezing (salt water, of course, freezes at a lower temperature than fresh water). Although not realised at the time, but subsequently discovered during metallurgical tests on samples taken from the wreck, it was exactly at this temperature that the *Titanic*'s steel plates were at their most brittle and therefore most vunerable to impact damage.

The figure walking aft on *Titanic*'s Promenade Deck is believed to be Captain Smith.

ABOVE: *Titanic*'s second class Promenade Deck.

LEFT: The impressive dressing table in Father Browne's stateroom on the *Titanic*.

TITANIC

High up ahead of the bridge, the two lookouts were probably concentrating as much on keeping warm as they did on trying to peer into the darkness ahead. Although there was no wind, the ship's speed would have been enough to send a bitingly cold draught though the rigging and the lookout's eyes would have been streaming in the chill air. For reasons never established, they had no binoculars, although they were standard aboard the *Olympic* and had been available in the *Titanic* as she sailed from Belfast to Southampton where they disappeared and were not seen again. No replacement pair was made available. Shortly after 11.30pm, less than half an hour before they were due to be relieved, the lookouts noticed an area of low lying mist ahead and the air became damp, adding to their discomfort. Silence descended as the two men peered intently ahead. Suddenly, without a word, Fleet tensed, leaned forward for a brief second and then reached across to give three sharp tugs on the lanyard which rang the 16in brass bell suspended above the crow's nest. As the sharp tones rang out, Fleet frantically grabbed the telephone linked directly to the bridge and twirled the ringer handle. Alerted by the warning bell, Sixth Officer James Moody picked up his receiver and heard the fatal message.

"Iceberg Right Ahead!"

RIGHT: Gym instructor T. W. McCawley tried to keep passengers calm by inviting them to use the gym equipment. He is shown here using the rowing machine. He went down with the ship. In the background can be seen Lawrence Beesley who survived and wrote one of the first books documenting the disaster.

FAR RIGHT: Father Browne's photograph of *Titanic*'s reading and writing room.

TITANIC

RIGHT: Passengers on A Deck aft, braving the inclement weather.

BELOW: American writer Jacques Futrelle outside the gymnasium, on *Titanic*'s Boat Deck.

TITANIC

LEFT: *Titanic*'s first class dining room in use.

BELOW: *Titanic*'s A Deck — the Verandah and Palm Court are through the sliding doors. The second class Promenade Deck can be seen at the top of the photograph.

TITANIC

RIGHT: *Titanic*'s port side, as she was seen at Queenstown in Ireland.

BELOW RIGHT: *Titanic* preparing to leave Queenstown after taking on board Irish emigrants heading for America.

BELOW: Irish emigrants crowding on the quayside waiting to board the tender to take them out to *Titanic*.

LEFT: Countess of Rothes viewing the tender arriving from Queenstown. Behind her is lifeboat No. 8 in which she escaped the sinking liner.

BELOW LEFT: The tender at Queenstown.

FOLLOWING PAGE: The tender passes under *Titanic*'s starboard wing bridge. Father Browne catches Captain Smith peering down.

TITANIC

LEFT: Captain Smith on the bridge of the *Titanic* at Southampton, April 10, 1912.
Artist: *Stuart Williamson*

BELOW: *Titanic* in the Thompson Graving Dock, Belfast, February, 1912.
Artist: *Stuart Williamson*

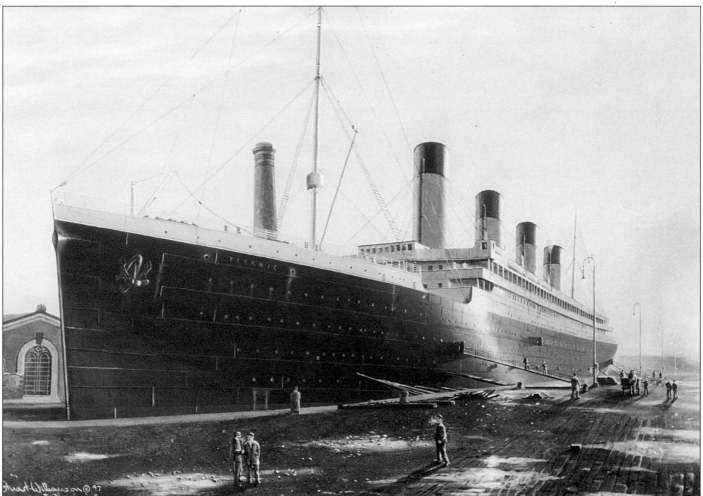

TITANIC

ABOVE LEFT: "The Last Meeting." *Titanic* and *Olympic* at Belfast, March, 1912.
Artist: *Simon Fisher*

LEFT: *Titanic* leaving Belfast, April 2, 1912.
Artist: *Stuart Williamson*

ABOVE and RIGHT: *Titanic* leaving Southampton, April, 10, 1912.
Artist: *Stuart Williamson*

TITANIC

LEFT: "Nightime Arrival."
Titanic at Southampton.
Artist: *Simon Fisher*

OVERLEAF: "A Close
Shave." *Titanic* leaving
Southampton.
Artist: *Simon Fisher*

TITANIC

RIGHT: "The Last Sunset." *Titanic* in the Atlantic.
Artist: *Simon Fisher*

OVERLEAF
ABOVE LEFT: "Iceberg Right Ahead."
Artist: *Simon Fisher*

BELOW LEFT: "1.45 a.m."
Artist: *Simon Fisher*

ABOVE RIGHT: "The Last Moments."
Artist: *Simon Fisher*

BELOW RIGHT: "The Breakup."
Artist: *Simon Fisher*

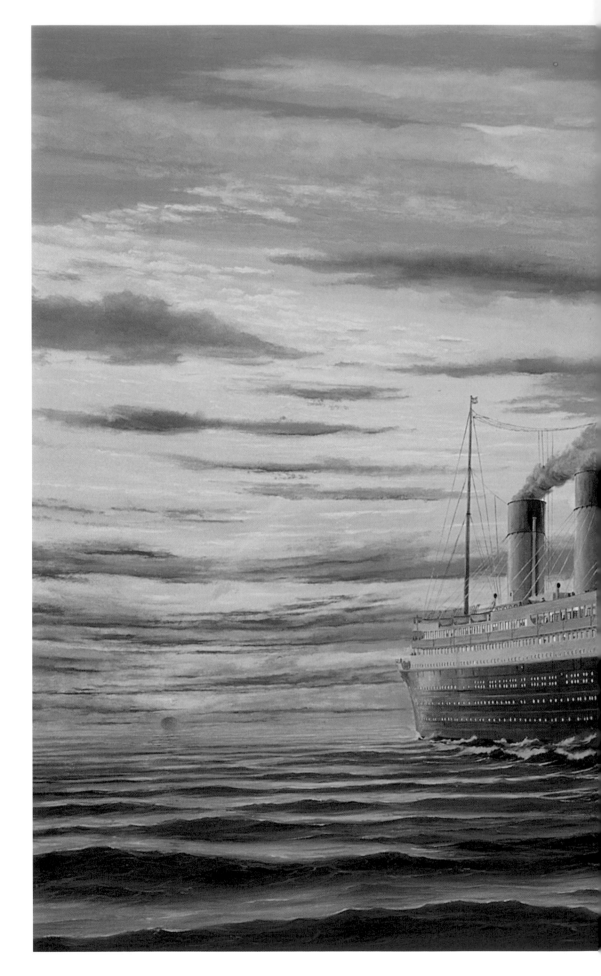

TITANIC

RIGHT: *"Carpathia* Picking
Up Survivors."
Artist: *Simon Fisher*

OVERLEAF: *Titanic*'s sister
ship, HMHS *Britannic,* en
route for the
Mediterranean, 1916.
Artist: *Stuart Williamson*

TITANIC

THIS PAGE: *Olympic*'s First Class lounge survived the ship's scrapping in 1936 and is now in a hotel in northen England.
Stephen Rigby

DEATH

TITANIC

PREVIOUS PAGE: Bruce Ismay escapes in one of the last lifeboats as portrayed in *A Night to Remember*.

BELOW: The launch of *Titanic* depicted in the film *A Night to Remember*. The launch was in reality a lower key affair without the usual champagne bottle-breaking.

As the *Titanic* sped through the darkness towards its doom, the majority of the passengers and crew had not the slightest inkling that they were in any danger at all. The lowering temperatures had long since driven the passengers off the promenade decks into the warmth of the saloons and cabins. Many had joined together to form their own groups and parties at dinner, one of which included the captain, and afterwards had dispersed to the smoke rooms, lounges and their own cabins. In the second class dining saloon, the Reverend E. C. Carter had organised a hymn service, attended by over a hundred passengers, which started at 8.00pm and lasted until after 10.00pm. By 11.30pm, just before the impact, most of the passengers had followed the captain's example and had retired to bed, leaving only a few stalwarts finishing their nightcaps and smoking a last cigar in the almost deserted smoking rooms and lounges.

On the bridge, the calm routine of the night was shattered by the warning bell from the crow's nest and Fleet's dramatic telephone call, although Sixth Officer Moody did not forget his manners as he thanked the lookout for his report before calling across the First Officer Murdoch, "Iceberg right ahead!"

Murdoch's reactions were creditably instantaneous. Leaping forward he grabbed the handles of the engine telegraph and rang down, "Stop," followed by, "Full Astern." At the same time he ordered the helmsman, Quartermaster Robert Hitchins, to turn the wheel "Hard-a-starboard." The order was obeyed promptly, Hitchens spinning the wheel as far as it would go, causing the ship to begin swinging to port (the apparent discrepancy between the helm order and the direction of the turn results from the system of orders in common use at that time which dated back to the days when ships were steered by a tiller, and pushing it to starboard resulted in a turn to port and vice versa — this system survived until the more logical current system was made standard in 1928). As the ship began to turn, Murdoch pressed the bell switch which warned all in the lower compartments that the watertight doors were about to close automatically, holding it down for 10 seconds before operating the lever to actuate the closure.

Despite the prompt reaction of all involved, the ship had only veered some 20 degrees to port when the fateful collision occurred. The interval between the first sighting and the

98

Walworth Road Baptist Church,
LONDON, S.E.
(Near Southwark Town Hall).

Pastor:
Rev. JOHN HARPER.

3, Claude Villas,
Love Walk,
Denmark Hill, S.E.

2nd April 1912

My Dear Brother Millican

I am to be in Walworth — God willing — after all, this weekend; as I received instructions this morning that my steamer the Lusitania cannot sail on Saturday, and as the steamer that goes in her place is a slow one I have decided to wait till next

Wednesday, and thus I am free to serve you on Monday and have arranged with dear Pastor Nillock to take the Service for you on that day. My earnest prayer is that every blessing shall Crown your lives in your union together. I will also be preaching on Sunday at 11 & 6.30. My Subject at 11 will be, "Did Christ rise Again?" at 6.30 Why was it Necessary?

With Kindest Christian love to your Father & Mother, Miss Adams & yourself.

Your Affectionate Pastor
John Harper

A letter written by the Reverend John Harper on 2 April 1912 informing friends that his passage on the *Lusitania* had been cancelled. The crucial part of the letter reads:
" . . . I am to be in Walworth — God willing — after all this weekend as I received instructions this morning that my steamer the *Lusitania* cannot sail on Saturday; and as the steamer that goes in her place is a slow one I have decided to wait till next Wednesday . . ."
Next Wednesday was *Titanic*'s sailing day and his decision sadly proved fatal as Reverend Harper would go down with the ship.

impact was later estimated to have been a little over 30 seconds, only enough time for the ship to cover some 500 yards and far too short to allow any successful avoiding action to be taken. Although a head-on collision had been averted, the starboard side of the *Titanic*'s hull crashed into the great mass of solid ice which then scraped relentlessly along the brittle underwater plating, leaving a trail of damage about 300ft long. In places it had gashed open the hull to a width of a few inches; in some points the hole was probably as little as half an inch wide. It was enough.

On the bridge, Fourth Officer Boxhall arrived on the bridge just as the collision occurred, having been due to take over watch a few minutes later. Almost immediately he was joined by the captain who had heard the warnings and felt the impact.

"What have we struck?" he asked the first officer anxiously. Murdoch quickly made his report, confirming that they had hit an iceberg and detailing the actions he had already taken. Both officers strode out onto the bridge wing to look aft for the iceberg and on re-entering the bridge the captain told Boxhall to inspect the forward area of the hull below decks and to report back as soon as possible. He moved the engine telegraphs to "Half Ahead," but then rang down "Stop," shortly afterwards. The *Titanic* slowed and then stopped dead in the water.

While the deck officers were uncertain as to the extent of the damage, if any, some of the stokers, firemen, trimmers and engineers unfortunate enough to have been on duty in the machinery spaces at the time had no doubts as to the seriousness of the situation. In the forward boiler room (No. 6), only two stokers and an engineer got out before the water began to rise and the watertight doors were closed. However, in the enginerooms further aft, the collision was only felt as a bump or a jar although the noise of the iceberg scrapping along the side was heard. In the ensuing 15 minutes Fourth Officer Boxhall made a quick tour of inspection in the forward hull and discovered that the Orlop Deck was flooded forward of No. 4 watertight bulkhead and, although he saw no water on F Deck, he was informed by the postal clerks that water was rising in the post office on the deck below. Returning quickly to the bridge he informed the captain of his findings and was then ordered to establish the ship's position so that it could be included in any subse-

A still from the film *Titanic* showing the tender taking passengers to the *Titanic* at Cherbourg.

quent wireless messages. Boxhall poured over the charts and calculated a dead reckoning position based on his own stellar observation at 7.30pm, updated with the ship's subsequent course and an estimate of its speed. Working under pressure, he quickly reported that the *Titanic* lay stopped at 41°46'N, 50°14'W, a position which became enshrined in maritime lore but was subsequently proved to be incorrect by a few vital miles, causing misunderstanding and controversy for decades afterwards.

While Boxhall worked at the chart table, Captain Smith went below to see things for himself and was accompanied by Thomas Andrews, the Harland & Wolff managing director, who probably knew as much as anybody about the ship and her construction. The latter did not take long to reach the unpalatable conclusion that the ship was mortally damage and estimated that it would sink an hour and a half, or two hours at the outside — a remarkably accurate assessment in the circumstances. One can only guess at how both men must have felt as the realisation dawned upon them. The main problem was the fact that the No. 6 boiler room was holed and that all the bow watertight compartments were also holed or filling. In this situation, it was only a matter of time before the bow sank low enough for water to lap over the top of the next watertight bulkhead, which only extended to E Deck, and into No. 5 boiler room. When this happened, the ship would settle even lower in the water and the other compartments would then flood in turn at successively shorter intervals. On his return to the bridge, a grim-faced captain ordered the crew to be mustered, the lifeboats uncovered, and the radio operators to begin transmitting a distress message using an approximate position, and this was first received at Cape Race and by at least two ships (*Mount Temple* and *Provence*) at 12.15am.

Once armed with Boxhall's new estimated position, accurate or not, the captain personally went to the radio room and ensured that it was included in all subsequent trans-

LEFT: The film's radio operator sends out the distress signal which was picked up over 50 miles away by the *Carpathia* which steamed over to rescue survivors from the icy sea.

BELOW: The real wireless room on *Titanic*, from which Harold Bride sent out the distress signal. The *Titanic* was equipped with state of the art 5kW wireless telegraphy system, installed by the Marconi company. It was guaranteed to transmit over a radius of 350 miles. The company also supplied the operators to work the new equipment.

TITANIC

RIGHT: Captain Smith informs Ismay, White Star Line's director, that the ship is doomed, from the film *A Night to Remember*.

missions, beginning at 12.25am. The message, sent in morse code, took the form of the *Titanic's* calling code, MGY, then the letters CQ, which meant that it was addressed to "all ships," followed by the letter "D" indicating distress or danger. The resulting three letter group was often held to mean "Come Quick, Danger," but in fact the letters had no significance other than as outlined above. In 1908 the famous SOS signal was introduced, this being easier to send in morse code as it consisted of three dots, three dashes and three dots, but it was still not in common use by 1912. Later in the evening, Bride and Phillips started using the SOS code instead of CQD, one of the first times that it had been used in an emergency.

As the officers and crew were roused and assembled, they were ordered to inform the passengers and direct them to assemble on the boat decks. This turned out to be an extremely difficult task as there was no tannoy or public address system and the stewards and crew had to go round all the cabins, wakening those many occupants who had not been disturbed by the collision and urge them to put on their lifejackets and find their way up to the boats on the boat deck. This task was not made any easier by the cacophony of noise on the upper decks caused by steam escaping through safety valves as the main engines were closed down, this noise also causing problems for the radio operators in their cabin at the base of the fore funnel where they could barely hear the high pitched morse signals being transmitted. At first, most passengers were not unduly concerned, refusing to believe that such a fine ship could be in any imminent danger. Indeed, many first class passengers formed an orderly queue at the purser's office on C Deck where they withdrew jewellery and other valuable items deposited for safe keeping during the voyage. Others took no immediate action to dress themselves in warm clothing or to find their lifejackets, assuming that all would be well in the end. Those passengers who did heed the warning slowly made their way up to the Boat Deck and, for the most part, formed patient groups waiting to embark. In the meantime, the ship's musicians, led by Lancashireman Wallace Hartley, assembled in the first class lounge on A Deck and began playing a succession of popular ragtime tunes. Although intended to help calm the passengers, their actions perhaps succeeded too well as the melodies sounding out into the chill night air lent an air of unreality to the whole proceedings.

Chief Officer Wilde ordered the second officer to see to the preparation of the lifeboats. Lightoller made a round of the Boat Deck, assigning crew members to work the lowering mechanism and ensuring that each boat was uncovered and made ready for loading, although he too had difficulty due to the noise, most orders being passed on by hand signals. He quickly checked boats 4, 6 and 8 immediately abaft the bridge on the port side and then moved aft along the Boat Deck to where boats 10, 12, 14 and 16 were stowed, before working his way forward along the starboard side past boats 15,13,11, and 9 and then to 7, 5 and 3 back by the bridge. Boats 1 and 2, the emergency cutters, were already swung out, and work began to prepare the collapsible Englehardt boats for use if required. By 12.25am Captain Smith had accepted that his ship was lost and that a lifeboat evacuation was the only remaining course. Realising that there were nowhere near enough lifeboat places for all on board, he ordered that only women and children should be loaded at first. Lightoller then ordered the lifeboats to be swung out and personally supervised the loading of boats on the port side while First Officer Murdoch looked after the starboard side. The plan was to load and lower the forward boat on each side, numbers 4 and 5, and then work progressively aft, lowering each boat in turn as they filled. However progress was slow, partly due to the crew's unfamliarity with the equipment and the drills to be used, they having been given virtually no training or exercise in such skills up to the time of the sinking. In addition the officers appeared not have been briefed on the capacities of the boats and allowed many to be lowered away only half full under the mistaken impression that they could not be safely lowered when filled to capacity. Another problem was caused by the screens fitted to the foreward section of the promenades on A Deck which prevented passengers boarding boats lowered from the Boat Deck just above, as was intend-

TITANIC

ABOVE: Families were separated through the women and children only rule. From the film *A Night to Remember*.

RIGHT: Many women were reluctant to leave their husbands and the safety of the ship. Again from the film *A Night to Remember*.

ed. There was some delay before the tool to undo the screen windows was found by which time some of the boats had already been lowered.

Because of these and other problems, it was not until 12.45am that the first lifeboat was finally lowered into the freezing water. This was number 7 from the port side which was considerably less than half full, carrying a maximum of 28 people against its certified capacity of 65. The occupants included three crewmen, and at least 8 female and 10 male passengers — a reflection on the lack of urgency pertaining at that time as the male passengers would only have been allowed to board if no women and children had been waiting. Next in the water was lifeboat number 5 under the command of Third Officer Pitman and although some 41 survivors were on board, it was still nowhere near full. The launch of this boat had been accompanied by some drama as J. Bruce Ismay appeared and attempted to take charge, blustering out improbable orders to passengers and crew alike. He was quickly put in his place by Fifth Officer Lowe and disappeared out of sight. Pitman took charge of the two boats s they rowed away from the ship and subsequently played an unedifying part in the drama, later refusing to return and pick up more survivors from the water as the ship sank. On a more amusing note (with hindsight) one of the women passengers suffered two broken ribs when Dr. H.Frauenthal and his brother, observing that the boat which already contained his wife also had many empty berths, leapt into it as it was being lowered and landed heavily on the unfortunate Mrs. Annie Stengel. Despite this unfortunate incident all happily survived to tell the tale.

On the port side, Lightoller finally managed to get lifeboat number 6 away at around 12.55am with about 28 people on board (it is difficult accurately to determine the actual numbers in each boat as witnesses' accounts varied tremendously and no official count was made at the time the lifeboats were first picked up). All of these were women apart from two crew members and two male passengers, one of whom was a Major Arthur Peuchen, an amateur yachtsman who had volunteered to assist in the handling of the boat. In the event, the crew members proved to be of little use and it was left to the women to do most of the rowing. Significantly, as the boat was about to be lowered, Captain Smith ordered Quartermaster Hitchens who was in charge of the boat to make for another ship whose lights could be seen some five miles away off the *Titanic*'s starboard bow. This was the first of many sightings of one (or possibly more) unidentified vessels in the vicinity and whose existence, or otherwise, became the subject of much speculation and investigation in the aftermath of the sinking.

For various reasons, partly because Murdoch was slightly less strict about the interpretation of the women and children first order, and partly because of difficulties caused by the fact that ship was listing slightly to starboard, the boats on this side were generally got away more quickly. Next away was lifeboat number 3 which contained around 50 people, including many male passengers and approximately 15 crew as, apparently, there were no more women or children in the vicinity when it was ready to be lowered. An attempt was made to load more passengers from A Deck as it was lowered, but this was frustrated by the locked windows of the promenade screens. With the three full size forward starboard lifeboats away, Murdoch and Lowe moved forward and attempted to launch the number 1 cutter. This was achieved with some difficulty and it did not enter the water until around 1.10am and only carried a dozen people, despite have a capacity of 40. The occupants were mostly crew but also included Sir Cosmo and Lady Duff-Gordon and their secretary. Sir Cosmo subsequently achieved some notoriety as there is no doubt that he actually paid the crew members five pounds each, although the reason for doing so was hotly debated. Some alleged that he bribed the men to row away from the ship, ignoring other survivors' cries for help, so that it would not be overloaded or dragged down when the ship sank, while he stoutly maintained that the payment was in gratitude for the crews assistance and to cover the cost of their personal losses. Whatever the truth of either version, the story is typical of the many personal dramas which make the tale of the *Titanic* so endlessly fascinating. The seaman in charge of this boat, George Symons, was also one of

TITANIC

ABOVE: *Olympic*'s bridge, which was identical to *Titanic*'s.

RIGHT: Young Jack O'Dell gazes out over the *Titanic*'s side.

many witnesses who reported seeing the lights of another ship and started to head towards it although in this case he reported the lights as being on the *Titanic's* port bow.

Meanwhile, on the port side of the Boat Deck, Chief Officer Wilde joined Lightoller and they succeeded in getting lifeboat number 8 away with around four crewmen and 35 women aboard. Captain Smith again instructed the crew to row for a ship whose lights he thought he could see in the distance but before the boat was lowered another little drama was played out when Mrs. Ida Straus refused to leave her husband who, despite urgings to the contrary by other passengers and crew in view of his old age, refused all offers to be allowed to break the women and children first rule. This brave, but needless, stance resulted in both being drowned when the ship finally sank. The undoubted hero, or more correctl, heroine, of this boat was Lady Lucy-Noel Martha, Countess of Rothes, who steadfastly took turns at rowing and steering as well as comforting some of the other women who had lost their husbands. Back on the starboard side, Murdoch and Moody got boat number 9 away at around 1.20am with 56 people aboard, the highest total so far and including 8 crewmen, and 6 male passengers. Again, occupants though that they saw the lights of ship and attempted row towards them, but with no success. Almost at the same time, boat number 10 was lowered on the port side; this was also well loaded with 4 crew members, 41 women and 7 children, together with 2 male passengers who had slipped aboard while the officers in charge of embarkation were distracted.

As the urgency of the situation began to dawn on all concerned, the later boats tended to be filled to much nearer their nominal capacity and boat 11, lowered away from the starboard side at around 1.25am, was one of the most crowded, one estimate putting the total on board at 70 people, mostly women. Almost simultaneously, lifeboat 12 was launched on the portside but contained only 40 women passengers and 2 crew, several male passengers having been denied access. With these two boats in the water, exactly half of the available lifeboats had been launched and work continued apace to get the rest filled up and lowered away. But it was not only on the boatdecks that significant incidents and drama occurred.

Olympic's **Poop Deck with docking bridge. On** *Titanic* **this is where most people gathered as the ship sank.**

TITANIC

While most of the officers were busily engaged in supervising the preparation and lowering of the boats, Fourth Officer Boxhall remained on the bridge and was ordered by the captain to begin firing pyrotechnics known as socket signals, to attract the attention of a vessel whose lights were seen by all on the bridge. The socket signals were fired from a mortar attached to the bridge rail, and each rose up to 800ft into the air before exploding into a dozen slow falling brilliant white lights. The first was fired at 12.45am and a total of eight were eventually fired at roughly five-minute intervals, the last at around 1.20am. However the mystery vessel, estimated to have been some five or six miles away, appeared not respond to the signals and slowly turned to starboard and was last observed heading away off the *Titanic*'s port bow. Attempts to signal the vessel by means of the powerful morse signal lamp also met with no response. The identity of this vessel, if it actually existed, is one of the many mysteries of this fateful night but what is certain is that the distress signals were seen by another more distant vessel, the *Californian* which lay stopped in the icefield somewhere between 8 and 19 miles north of the *Titanic*. The actions of this ship and her commander, Captain Stanley Lord, became the centre of much controversy and speculation in the aftermath of the sinking and Lord was accused of virtually ignoring the drama supposedly unfolding before his very eyes.

While these various scenes were being enacted on the bridge and boat decks, activity below was varied and stories from surviving witnesses are necessarily fragmented. Often told is the cool example of a Colonel Gracie who on recognising Frederick Wright, the professional squash player, calmly requested that his booking for Monday morning be cancelled! In the third class saloons, many of the Catholic Irish emigrants came together and recited their rosary as they awaited their fate. There were undoubted cases of both passengers and crew helping themselves to gin or brandy, or whatever they could lay their hands on, and drinking whole bottles to blot out what was happening but, on the whole such instances were uncommon, and most passengers queued stoically for the boats or else waited patiently in the saloons still perhaps hoping that the ship would not really sink. However, down below events were moving quickly to seal the vessel's fate. In number 5 boiler room a few firemen and engineers remained to man the pumps in an attempt to stop the compartment flooding but suddenly, at around 12.45am, the bulkhead between 5 and 6 boiler rooms gave way and the whole compartment was flooded within seconds. Only one occupant, Leading Stoker Fred Barrett, managed to escape; all the others were drowned. It has been suggested that the collapsing bulkhead could have been damaged by the bunker fire which was burning when the ship left Belfast.

Up on deck the work of filling and lowering the boats continued. Following on the experiences of those already described was boat number 14 from the port side. This is believed to have contained 63 people, all but 10 of them women, and was under the command of Fifth Officer Lowe who had been ordered to take charge by the chief officer. Once in the water, Lowe had the boat rowed away from the ship and gathered a number of other boats together. He than transferred most of the passengers out of his boat with the intention of rowing back and picking up more survivors although, by the time he was ready to carry out this plan, there were few left alive in the bitterly cold water to be rescued. On the starboard side, boats 13 and 15 were launched one after the other with around 63 and 70 people aboard respectively. As the first of these entered the water and drifted slightly sternwards while still attached to the falls, the second boat was almost lowered on top of it, disaster only being averted when those seaman lowering the boat heard screams from below and stopped its descent. In fact boat 15 was one of the few to carry significant numbers of third class passengers who otherwise had proportionately fewer survivors than amongst first or second class passengers. Subsequent inquiries looked at this point in some detail and it was accepted that there were no physical obstacles to prevent third class passengers accessing the boat decks, but that it would have been difficult for many of them to have found their way around the unfamiliar parts of the ship in the cir-

TITANIC

cumstances. With the first class accommodation just below the Boat Deck, it was obviously much easier for these passengers to reach the lifeboats, although there were many examples of crew members going below and making efforts to guide other passengers up from the lower decks.

By now the ship was well down by the bows and had taken a slight list. Nevertheless boat 16, the last of the standard lifeboats on the starboard side, was launched without trouble carrying some 56 passengers and crew. First Officer Murdoch then went forward and began to prepare boat C, one of the collapsible boats, for launching. This had a flat wooden bottom and canvas side which could be raised and rigged to give a freeboard of around three feet. The launch of this boat was not without excitement and Murdoch at one stage fired his pistol into the air in order to hold back a group of men who tried to rush aboard. When it finally got away, estimates of the numbers aboard varied from a wildly exaggerated 70 to a more generally accepted figure of 39, many of whom were women passengers from third class. The most controversial occupant was J. Bruce Ismay, the White Star Line chairman who subsequently stated that he stepped aboard only because there were no other passengers waiting in the vicinity, while other witnesses claimed that he pushed through a crowd of men in order to force himself aboard. Whatever the truth, the poor man was subsequently vilified by unsympathetic commentators who obviously thought that he should have followed the example of the captain and gone down with the ship — although what would have been achieved by such a sacrifice is open to question.

Boat 2, one of the emergency cutters, was launched at 1.45am and was under the command of hard working Fourth Officer Boxhall, who had the presence of mind to equip himself with some green signal rockets so that, subsequently, his was the first boat to be located and picked up. There were only 26 in the cutter and it was eventually followed by lifeboat number 4, the last of the standard boats, at 1.55am. The launch of this had been one of the epics of the night, as it was one of the first to be prepared and had been low-

TOP LEFT: Desperate passengers struggling to escape, a scene on *Titanic*'s deck, from the film *Atlantic*.

BELOW LEFT: Even at the last, some gamblers are trying to distract themselves from their imminent death. A fictitious scene on the *Titanic;* again from *Atlantic*.

Below: Another scene from the film *Atlantic*.

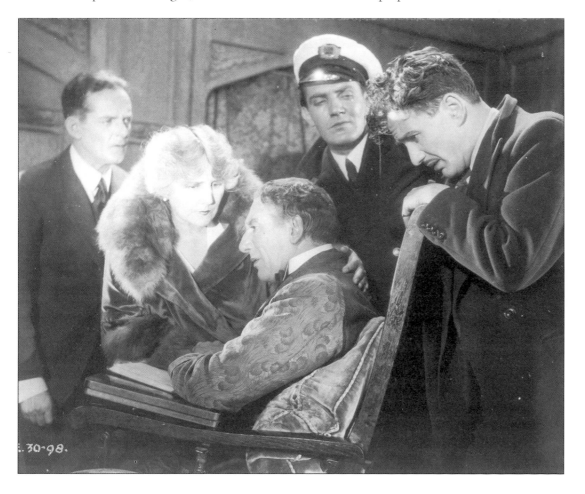

ered on Lightoller's instructions, to A Deck level so that passengers could board. Unfortunately he had forgotten about the locked screens and had it hauled up again, before it was again lowered back and efforts made to undo the screens. While all this was going on, a most orderly and genteel queue of first class women passengers, together with their children and maids, waited patiently on the promenade. By the time that the boat was ready for loading, the ship's list had carried it away from the side and a cable was used to pull it in close enough for the women to step across. Eventually some 36 were safely aboard, and these were later joined by four crewman (and one stowaway). Observing that the boat was still not full, the multimillionaire Colonel Astor asked Lightoller if he might join his wife in the lifeboat but permission was refused. Forever the gentleman, Astor did not argue and stood back as his young bride disappeared into the darkness below. He did not survive.

Finally attention turned the to collapsible boat D which was lowered from davits on the port side and was virtually full with around 46 people on board. As it was launched, at 2.05am, the *Titanic*'s forecastle was almost completely submerged, water was lapping around B Deck further aft and the ship's stern was noticeably beginning to lift out of the sea. The only boats remaining now were the two collapsibles, A and B, on the roof of the officers' accommodation at the base of the fore funnel. As officers and crew members struggled to release these, the ship began to sink rapidly beneath them and both floated off as a tide of water washed around and over the bridge, neither of them properly rigged and boat B ending up inverted. Nevertheless some 30 men managed to climb onto the upturned hull while around 20 swam to boat A which had enough buoyancy to float even though the canvas screens had not been erected.

The *Titanic* was now in its final death throes, but still the various dramas were being acted out. Although the captain had relieved them of their duties some time earlier, the two radio operators stayed at their posts until the last possible moment, Phillips still trying to transmit up to 2.17am, only minutes before the ship sank. Benjamin Guggenheim, one of the richest passengers, watched the women and children get away in the boats and then

RIGHT: The crew members know that they are doomed when water enters the boiler room. From the film *Titanic*.

FAR RIGHT: Lifeboats leave the stricken liner. From the film *Titanic*, made in 1953.

TITANIC

How the rescue was reported at the time in *The Sphere* 4 May 1912. Published weekly for 6d.

How the "Titanic" Survivors were Picked Up

"Titanic" Lifeboat Seen from the "Carpathia's" Side

Collapsible Boat Containing some

The Boats of the "Titanic" Hanging on the "Carpathia's" Sides

"Titanic" Survivors being Waited on by "Carpathia" Passengers

A Boatload of   She

e "Carpathia" : Direct Photographic Pictures by Mr. J. W. Barker, a Passenger on the "Carpathia."

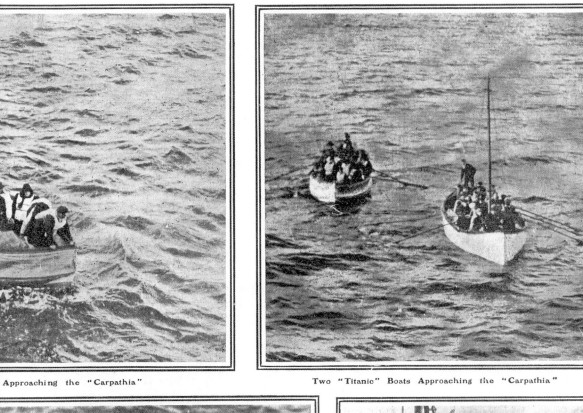

Approaching the "Carpathia"

Two "Titanic" Boats Approaching the "Carpathia"

and Women and Seamen with Oars

Fixing a Rope Step Ladder from the Boat to the "Carpathia"

FAR LEFT: A photograph of Father Thomas Roussell Byles, who gave absolution and heard confessions as the *Titanic* sank.

LEFT: Lifeboats leave the stricken ship, from the film Atlantic.

retired with his valet to his cabin, reappearing later in full evening dress saying that he was prepared to go down like a gentleman. On the after deck, Catholic priest Thomas Byles was hearing confessions, while in the first class saloon a foursome made up of Major Archie Butt and three friends played cards until well after two o'clock. Thomas Andrews, the Harland & Wolff managing director, sat in the first class smoking room staring at a painting on the wall and was not seen again. On the bridge, the captain was at his post as it was engulfed by the rising sea and, all the time, the ship's musicians played on but, as the bow began to slip under the waves they stopped the cheerful ragtime music which had lent such an air of unreality to the occasional and struck up with a traditional hymn, "Nearer, My God, to Thee." Several survivors attest that their last piece was another hymn, "Autumn,",but the former was known to be a favourite of the bandleader, Hartley, and is the most probable rendition to have been played at this poignant moment.

As the bow went under, the ship began to tilt down rapidly, the stern rising into the air, spilling people into the sea while, at the same moment, the ship's lights suddenly went out after having burned brightly throughout the night thanks to the efforts of a dedicated band of engineers who had kept up enough steam to drive the generators. As the ship was dragged down by its flooded forward section, the hull rose almost vertically, the fore funnel breaking off and falling amongst swimmers in the water. She hung in that attitude for several seconds before commencing the plunge to the ocean floor over 12,000ft below. As the mighty vessel finally went down, it was accompanied by a rising crescendo of noise as furniture and fittings crashed about inside the hull, coal shifted in the bunkers and hot boilers split and exploded on contact with the ice-cold water. But, suddenly, all was silent and the ship had disappeared forever, taking with it over 1,000 people and leaving others drowning in its ice-cold wake. All that was left were the lifeboats, bobbing in the gradually settling waves, floating in a scene of Arctic desolation lit only by the stars in the clear sky above. The time was 2.20am, 2hr 40min from the time that the iceberg ripped into the *Titanic*'s hull.

TITANIC

Alfred Fernand on his oath saith as follows

I am a cotton agent at Havre. I joined the Titanic at Cherbourg on the 10th April as a 1st class passenger. We had good weather all the way till the disaster, and at the time of the disaster.

On Sunday the 14th April so far as I know there was no boat drill — I am practically sure.

The captain was in the Saloon at dinner on Sunday night the 14th April. Afterwards, after dinner there was the Orchestra in the Companion-way and the Captain was there. This was on the 'D' deck. The 'A' deck was on the 1st deck down from the top deck. Monsieur Marechal remarked to me that the Captain was with a party and seemed very happy and very confident in his boat. Then we went and played Bridge in the 'Café Parisien'. We played on until about 11.40pm and then there was a shock. I have crossed the Atlantic 13 times, and the shock was not a great one, and I thought it was caused by a wave. After about a few minutes I asked the waiter to put down the port-hole, and he did so, and we saw nothing. When the shock had happened, we saw something white through the port-holes, and we saw water on the ports. When the waiter opened the   port-hole we saw nothing except a clear night.

About a minute after the waiter had opened the port holes we all left the café. Marechal put the cards in his jacket, and so did I — I went all round to find my friends to go on with the game. We waited a very long time, and everybody told us there was nothing at all. About 12.30 we saw the Captain and the 1st officer going up to the bridge. All around about 50 or 60 women and men were waiting anxiously to know what was happening. The Captain came down with the 1st officer. The Captain was chewing a toothpick and he said 'You had better put your life-preservers on, as a precaution.' Then I went down to my cabin, a few floors down, and I put my life-belt on. Then I went up to the boat deck, and it was deadly cold. I came back to my own cabin, took off my life-belt and put on my overcoat. Then I came up, and put on again my life-belt. I was then on the boat deck. I saw them get down some boats. While I was still on the boat deck, a boat was let down. The 1st officer saw me and asked me if I wanted to get in. Some of the passengers shouted to me not to get in as they had such confidence in the ship. I saw that the sea was very calm, and on calm reason I thought it better to jump into the boat and see what would happen. I jumped two or three yards, and landed in the boat anyhow. We were twenty nine in the boat. the boat could not have held more than thirty in any case. I personally consider and state that the idea of putting sixty people in a boat or on a raft is ridiculous. I have a photograph in my possession which shows how ridiculous it is to attempt to put 50 or sixty persons in one of these boats or rafts. I consider it a monstrosity to state that one could put 60 persons in a boat in safety.

When we were being lowered, about 125yds from the sea, a man put one rope much lower than the other one and we nearly went over. Then we went down and touched water. Then it was difficult to get free and we had to cut the rope to get free.

When we were in the water we started to row away from the ship. I was rowing. We had about 22 women on board. Marechal my friend was on board, and I did not recognise him till the morning. We rowed up to about 150 yards from the ship. We saw the ship sink gradually — she sank to starboard.

We had no lights in our lifeboat, no compass, no chart, but we had a small cask of water, and I heard that we had a small box of biscuits. After the ship had gone down and before, we saw a light far off, about eight or ten miles. Everyone thought it was another ship — a sailing or steam boat. We saw it plainly. We all cheered up, thinking we were going to be saved; we saw it gradually disappear.

We thought it was either a sailing boat that could not move on account of the very calm weather, or else an optical illusion on our part.

Then we waited until dawn: then the Carpathia came up. We were royally treated on board the Carpathia. Any man who was saved by the Carpathia will always have in his own mind the faces of the captian and officers. I know personally how much the captain of the Carpathia had at heart to save the Titanic.

One of the lookout men was in our boat. He told us that he had seen the iceberg about three mintues before the shock. I am no sailor, but if he did so, we must take into consideration that the ship was going 20 miles an hour at least, ie, he saw the iceberg 1760 yards (and advised it) before meeting it.

I consider as a passenger, that two people knew that the icebergs were around us — these two are the head of the company and the Captain — I ask, how is it that neither of those two said a word for the safety of the passengers? We passengers always consider that we have to deliver our own safety to the captain, and therefore have a right to know if our life is properly looked after, and if in case of records for speed we have to risk it for the benefit of companies.

After the disaster, the captain and officers behaved like gentlemen.

**Sworn by the said Alfred Fernand Omont
in the presence of
James Walsh.
British Vice Consul
Havre**

AFTERMATH

TITANIC

Much of the controversy surrounding the sinking of the *Titanic* focused on the actions of other ships in the vicinity at the time. Mention has already been made of lights seen by both passengers and crew but the vessel concerned has never been positively identified, if indeed there actually was a ship so close and the lights observed were not stars — a mistake made on many other occasions, even by experienced observers. One possible candidate was the 506grt Norwegian sailing barque, *Samson*, whose chief officer made a sworn statement in 1962 shortly before his death. He stated that he had seen the *Titanic*'s distress rockets but that the barque had altered course and sailed away as she had previously been engaged in an illegal sealing expedition off the Canadian coast and feared that the rockets were a signal to heave to so that she could be boarded and inspected. While this story could be true, there was no other corroborative evidence and official records show the ship to be in Icelandic waters at the time. It is known that a Massachusetts fishing schooner, the *Dorothy Baird*, was somewhere near the scene of the sinking but it cannot be established that she was actually within visual range on the night in question. Neither of these vessels carried a radio and their small size would have limited the number of survivors which they could have rescued even if they had realised what was going on.

The ship which was caught up in the backlash of public opinion and the widespread desire to find a scapegoat was the cargo liner *Californian* and her unfortunate Captain, Stanley Lord. This 6,223grt steamer had been launched in 1901 and was owned by the Leyland line, itself one of many taken over by International Mercantile Marine who also owned the White Star Line and the *Titanic* itself. She had sailed from Liverpool on April 5, 1912, carrying a general cargo to Boston and by noon on the fateful April 14 was at position 42°05'N, 47°25'W. In view of the ice warnings received by his radio operator, Captain Lord decided to alter course to pass slightly south of his originally planned course. Despite this, large icebergs were spotted at 6.30pm, still to the south of the ship, and this information was passed by radio to another Leyland ship, the *Antillian*, at 7.30pm. The *Californian*'s radio operator (Cyril Evans) subsequently established that this signal had also been picked up by the *Titanic*. Concerned about the proximity of the icefield, Lord stationed himself on the bridge and doubled his lookouts. At around 10.15pm he ordered the ship to stop when a glow in the darkness ahead was interpreted as a possible icefield and decided to heave to for the night, the position being recorded in the log as 42°05'N, 50°7'W. If Boxhall's estimate of the *Titanic*'s position were correct, then the *Californian* had stopped at a point just under 20 miles NNE from where the tragedy was to occur.

At around 10.30pm the masthead lights of a ship approaching from the east were seen and Lord checked with his wireless operator to see if he was aware of any other ships in the vicinity. On being told that the only known vessel was the *Titanic*, he ordered Evans to advise the latter that the *Californian* was stationary in an icefield although, as we have seen, this message was brushed aside by the recipient's operators. Having been on continuous duty since 7.00am that morning, Evans shut down his radio and went off duty shortly after this exchange as there was no requirement at that time that ships should maintain a continuous listening watch. An hour later, the other vessel appeared to be passing some five miles to the south and Third Officer Groves attempted to establish contact by signal lamp, but no answer was forthcoming. Over half an hour later, just after midnight, Second Officer Stone thought that he saw the lights of another ship, this time heading east, but again no contact was established. Shortly afterwards Captain Lord retired to the chart room for a rest, leaving orders that he was to be called if anything unusual occurred. Between 12.45am and 1.15am, Stone observed what he took to be signal rockets in the distance, in line with the vessel which he had previously seen and which now appeared to be stationary, although his report indicated that he did not consider that the lights actually came from the vessel which he could see. After observing the rockets he called down the voicepipe to the captain who requested to be kept informed of any developments. Subsequently James Gibson, a young cadet, was sent down to report that more rockets had been fired and that

Transcript of Register for Transmission to Registrar-General of Shipping and Seamen.

Official Number	Name of Ship	No., Date, and Port of Registry
131,428	Titanic	1912 Liverpool

No., Date, and Port of previous Registry (if any) new vessel

Whether British or Foreign Built	Whether a Sailing or Steam Ship; and if a Steam Ship, how propelled	Where Built	When Built	Name and Address of Builders
British	Steamship Triple Screw	Belfast	1912	Harland and Wolff Ltd Belfast

		Feet	Tenths
Number of Decks ... five & two partial	Length from fore part of stem, under the bowsprit, to the aft side of the head of the stern post	852	5
Number of Masts ... two	Length at quarter of depth from top of weather deck at side amidships to bottom of keel	849	2
Rigged ... Schooner			
Stern ... Elliptical	Main breadth to outside of plank plating	92	5
Build ... clencher	Depth in hold from tonnage deck to ceiling at midships	31	6
Galleries ...	Depth in hold from upper deck to ceiling at midships, in the case of three decks and upwards	59	5.8
Head ...	Depth from top of beam amidships to top of keel	64	9.1
Framework and description of steel vessel	Depth from top of deck at side amidships to bottom of keel	65	3.3
Number of Bulkheads ... fifteen	Round of beam ...		9.8
Number of water ballast tanks seventeen	Length of engine room, if any		
and their capacity in tons ... 5,426 Tons			

PARTICULARS OF DISPLACEMENT.

Total to quarter the depth from weather deck at side amidships to bottom of keel ... 77,480 Tons. Ditto per inch immersion at same depth ... 165 Tons.

PARTICULARS OF PROPELLING ENGINES, &c. (if any).

No. of sets of Engines	Description of Engines	Whether British or Foreign made	When made	Name and address of makers	No. and Diameter of Cylinders in each set.	Length of Stroke.	No. of Cylinders in each set.	N.H.P. I.H.P. Speed of Ship.
Two	Two Cylinder triple expansion inverted vertical direct acting surface condensing	British	1912	Harland & Wolff Ltd	1-54" 1-84	48		6906 150,000
					2-97"			21 knots

No. of Shafts	Description of Boilers				
Three	Number 29	British	1912	Belfast	

PARTICULARS OF TONNAGE.

GROSS TONNAGE.	No. of Tons	DEDUCTIONS ALLOWED.	No. of Tons
Under Tonnage Deck ...	17,840.66	On account of space required for propelling power ...	21,687.68
Space or spaces between Decks lower upper middle	14,142.81	On account of spaces occupied by Seamen or Apprentices, and appropriated to their use, and kept free from Goods or Stores of every kind, not being the personal property of the Crew :—	
Turret or Trunk ...		These spaces are the following, viz.:—	
Forecastle ...	270.29	In lower middle upper and saloon tween decks poop forecastle bridge and round houses	2628.96
Bridge space ...	3633.45		
Poop or Break ...	294.21		
Side Houses ...			
Deck Houses ...	3702.89	Deductions under Section 79 of the Merchant Shipping Act, 1894, and Section 54 of the Merchant Shipping Act, 1906, as follows:—	
Chart House ...			
Spaces for machinery, and light, and air, under Section 78 (2) of the Merchant Shipping Act, 1894	1184.16	Fore peak water ballast tank 44.43 after " 20.95	148.89
Excess of Hatchways ...		Master's accommodation 21.96 Boatswain's stores 48.00 Chart Room 6.23	
Gross Tonnage	46,328.57 131,107.86		
Deductions, as per Contra	24,497.23 67,324.16		
Register Tonnage	21,831.34 61,782.64	Total	24,497.23

NOTE.—1. The tonnage of the engine room spaces below the upper deck is 11,203.94 tons, and the tonnage of the total spaces framed in above the upper deck for propelling machinery and for light and air is 1184.16 tons.

NOTE.—2. The undermentioned spaces above the upper deck are not included in the cubical contents forming the ship's register tonnage : Open space in front of poop 16 feet long = 65.24 Tons Open space abaft 2nd class smoke room 6 ft long = 15.84 Tons Open space on Promenade deck, abreast windows, port side - 198 feet long = 343.27 Tons. Open " " Starbd " 198 " 347.22 "

Name of Master		Certificate of { Service No. { Competency No.

Names, Residence, and Description of the Owners, and Number of Sixty-fourth Shares held by each ... viz.,

Oceanic Steam Navigation Company Limited having its principal place of business at 30 James Street Liverpool } Sixty four Shares

of Harold Arthur Sanderson 30 James Street, Liverpool designated Manager

Advice received 25th day of March 1912.

Under the seal of the owning Company

Dated 25th March 1912. W. H. Ingram Registrar.

NOTE.—Registrars in the Colonies are requested to distinguish the Managing Owner by placing the letters "M.O." against his name.

N.B.—To be sent in an envelope addressed to the Registrar-General of Shipping and Seamen, Tower Hill, London, E.

the previously stationary vessel had now disappeared. However Lord does not seem to have been fully awake and the cadet was obviously apprehensive at disturbing his stern captain, and retired after an inconclusive exchange. This version of events, as told by the officers on the bridge, was slightly at variance with evidence subsequently given by a fireman, Ernest Gill, who claimed that he had come on deck at midnight after four hours on duty below and saw a very large steamer passing about 10 miles away off the starboard side. He then went below but returned to the deck 30 minutes later when he saw two white rock-

TITANIC

Discharge book from the *Titanic* crew survivor Percival Albert Blake. This shows that the surviving crew members were only paid until the ship sank. The book also shows that Percival Blake served on *Titanic*'s sister ship *Olympic* as a trimmer on the transatlantic run.

	P. A. Blake		11 CERTIFICATE	OF DISCHARGE. 12		P. A. Blake	
No.	*Name of ship and official number, Port of registry, and tonnage.†	*Date and place of engagement.	*Rating ; and R.N.R. No. (if any).	Date and place of discharge.	Description of voyage.	Signature of Master.	
13	Olympic 131346 Liverpool - 20846	20 Dec 1911 Southampton	Trimmer	6 Jan 1912 Southampton	New York		
14	D.º	10 Jan 1912 Southampton	Trimmer	31 Jan 1912 Southampton	D.º		
15	D.º	7 Feb 1912 Southampton	Trimmer	28 Feb 1912 Southampton	D.º	Extracted from Agreement	Registrar General 23rd May 1912
16	D.º	13 Mar 1912 Southampton	Trimmer	30 Mar 1912 Southampton	D.º		
17	Titanic 131428 Liverpool - 21831	10 Apr 1912 Southampton	Trimmer	15 Apr 1912 At Sea	Intended New York.		
18							

* These columns are to be filled in at time of engagement.   † In Engineers' Books Insert Horse Power.   680461

ets within the space of a few minutes, again off to starboard. He did not notify the bridge of these sightings, nor did he see any morse lamp signals from the other ship nor hear any noises, such as the concussion from the exploding rockets.

And so the night passed, the officers and crew of the *Californian* blissfully unaware of the drama which had actually occurred only a few miles away. However when daylight came, Captain Lord returned to the bridge in order see if passage through the ice was possible. His attention was drawn to a four-masted vessel with a yellow funnel off to the south southeast and it was thought that this might have been the one which had fired rockets during the night. Concerned that the vessel might require assistance, Lord roused his radio operator and ordered him to attempt to raise the other ship. As Evans tuned his equipment and transmitted a standard CQ message, he was startled to receive a reply from the *Frankfurt*, a 7,431grt German liner, asking if they were aware that the *Titanic* had struck an iceberg and sunk during the night. This was followed by confirmation from the *Virginian*, a 10,757grt British ship, which also passed the all-important position of the sinking. Lord and his chief officer plotted this on their charts, realising as they did so that they were very close to the sinking and possibly able to assist with the search for survivors. The captain immediately ordered the ship to get underway, the time being now around 5.30am, and pushed cautiously though the ice at 6kts before reaching open water on the west side and pushing southward at the *Californian*'s maximum speed of 13kts. After another hour she passed the Canadian Pacific liner *Mount Temple* which lay stopped at the reported position of the sinking although there were no wreckage or survivors to be seen. Continuing southward, the *Californian* eventually sighted the Cunard liner *Carpathia* to the southeast, on the other side of the icefield, and learned by wireless that the latter was at the actual position of the sinking and was even then picking up survivors. The two ships eventually came together at 8.30am, indicating that the *Californian* must have been at least 25 miles from the scene when the *Titanic* sank.

Although Captain Lord subsequently became something of a scapegoat, his was not the only ship which might have been within visual range of the *Titanic* during the night at the time of the sinking. The 6,661grt Canadian Pacific liner *Mount Temple* under the command of Captain James Moore was sailing from Antwerp to New York and was approximately 49 miles southwest when it picked up the *Titanic's* first distress signals at around 12.15am. Captain Moore immediately altered course to the northeast but shortly after 3.00am he began to encounter ice and then suddenly had to put his engines in reverse and turn hard to port in order to avoid a collision with a schooner sighted just ahead. After this incident he continued cautiously forward, stopping occasionally, before reaching the reported position of the *Titanic* at 4.30am. No wreckage or lifeboats were seen, and the captain later stated that no signals or rockets had been observed during the night, although an unidentified tramp steamer had been observed steaming on a similar course for some time. When daylight came, he continued searching until approximately 9.00am when he became aware that the survivors had been rescued. It will be remembered that the *Mount Temple* was sighted by the *Californian* she headed towards the area of the sinking during the early hours of the 15th, which would indicate that the *Mount Temple* had actually been much closer to the sinking than the latter. Despite her captain's assertions, at least two people (one passenger and one ship's officer) on the *Mount Temple* made statements to the effect that the *Titanic's* lights and signals had indeed been sighted but that the *Mount Temple* stood off and made no attempt to move closer until well after daybreak. For some reason, the account and actions of Captain Moore were never seriously challenged and he avoided the destructive publicity directed at Captain Lord.

In contrast to the relatively quiet night passed by the *Californian* and *Mount Temple*, the *Carpathia* had been a shining example of efficiency and properly directed action which had resulted in her being the only ship to arrive in time to pick up the living survivors. The credit for this rested entirely with her captain, Arthur Rostron, who had joined the Cunard Line in 1895 and rose to his first command in 1907, taking over the 13,603grt *Carpathia* in January 1912. This ship had left New York at noon on April 11, 1912, with 743 passengers, fortunately only a fraction of her designed accommodation for around 2,200, bound for Gibraltar and then on to other Mediterranean ports. On the fateful Sunday the *Carpathia's* only radio operator, 21-year old Harold Cottam, had been on duty continuously since 7.00am that morning and, as midnight approached, he was preparing to close down his radio and retire to bed. While undressing he kept his headphones on, listening out for a reply to an earlier communication which he had addressed to the liner *Parisian* although this was not forthcoming. While he waited, he idly retuned to the Cape Cod frequency and heard several messages addressed to the *Titanic* which he noted down with the intention of passing them on when the opportunity occurred. He then continued his preparations for bed when, on an impulse, he decided to see if he could raise the liner himself. The time was almost 12.30am

His message to the *Titanic* was phrased in the jargon favoured by radio operators of the day. Using the *Carpathia's* callsign MPA, he started tapping his morse key.

"I say, Old Man, do you know there is a batch of messages coming through for you from MCC (code for Cape Cod)?"

Even before he had finished, the *Titanic* broke in with an electrifying message of her own: "MGY (*Titanic*), Come at once. We have struck an iceberg. It's CQD, Old Man. Position 41°46'N, 50°14'W."

Cottam quickly ascertained that this was a genuine message and dashed, half-dressed, to the bridge to report the exchange to the first officer who immediately conducted him down to the captain's cabin where Rostron had just retired for the night. Instantly wide awake, the latter rushed up to the chart room and quickly determined that his ship was some 58 miles southeast of the *Titanic's* reported position. His subsequent actions were those of a professional master mariner who knew his trade inside out and needed no prompting to do what was necessary. As the *Carpathia* swung round onto a course of 308° to close the *Titanic*, he ordered the ship's 18 lifeboats to be prepared and swung out while the chief engineer was asked to raised maximum steam, shutting down much ancillary machinery and heating systems in order to ensure no steam was wasted. As a result of some Herculean efforts by the stokers, the *Carpathia* eventually worked up to a speed of 17.5kts, a speed that does not sound particularly impressive until it is realised that the ship's designed maximum speed under favourable conditions was only 14.5kts! As the hull quivered and vibrated under this extra strain, the entire crew was briefed to prepare to receive survivors, but not before every man was served with a hot drink to fortify them for the work ahead. Passengers were asked to remain calm and keep to their cabins so as not to hinder the crew as they cleared spaces, piled up blankets, and made the boats ready. Hot soup and drinks were prepared and arrangements made to accommodate the people from the *Titanic* as they came aboard, while the three doctors aboard were alerted and made their own preparations. Lights were rigged to illuminate the ship's side, while ladders, lines and tackle were made ready to gather survivors from the lifeboats. Barrels of oil were made available so that rough waters could, if necessary be calmed to assist the lifeboats coming alongside.

As the *Carpathia* tore through the night, additional lookouts were posted and all eyes strained forward in the darkness. Meanwhile Cottam was back at his post in the radio room listening to the *Titanic's* increasingly desperate radio transmissions, each of which was relayed to his captain by a steward acting as a messenger. The last one which he recorded was received at 1.45am, stating "Engine Room full up to the boilers." Only 45 minutes later a green flare was sighted in the distance far ahead. This, it transpired, had been fired by Boxhall from lifeboat number 2. Rostron ordered rockets to be fired at 15-minute intervals so that any survivors would know that rescue was approaching although it was almost another hour before the *Carpathia* reached the reported position of the sinking, and at that time no boats or wreckage had been spotted. However there were occasional glimpses of green lights low in the water ahead and these eventually turned out to be those of the lifeboats. At 4.00am, just before dawn broke, Captain Rostron order the engines to "Stop" and the *Carpathia* drifted to a halt only a few hundred yards from Boxhall's boat. Ten minutes later it lay under the *Carpathia's* starboard side and the work of getting the 25 occupants aboard began. Boxhall himself, still suffering from exposure to the cold and from shock, was taken to the bridge where he was able to give a brief account of what had happened, confirming to the disbelieving listeners that the *Titanic* had indeed been lost.

As the thin daylight began to illuminate the scene, the scale and nature of the catastrophe slowly became apparent. The *Titanic's* lifeboats with their pitiful survivors rode the barely disturbed sea while the whole area was strewn with icebergs of all shapes and sizes,

The first radio message received at 11.45pm by the SS *Birma* of the Russian East Asiatic SS Co. The message begs for help after hitting the iceberg. *Titanic* gives her position as Lat 41°46'N, Long 50°14'W. The *Birma* was about 100 miles southwest of *Titanic* when her radio operator received this distress call from MYG — *Titanic's* call sign.

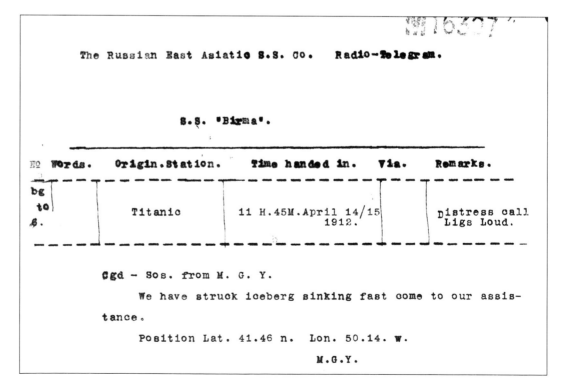

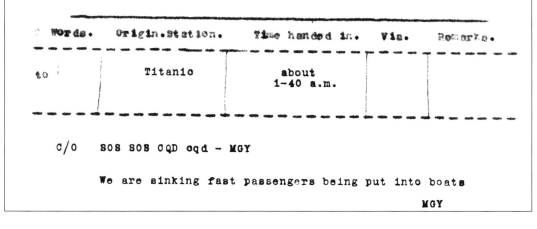

After asking for further information the radio operator on *Birma* received this desperate communication from *Titanic* at about 1.40am:
'We are sinking fast passengers being put into boats.'

the largest towering more than 200ft above the water. Fortunately the calm conditions meant that the lifeboats had mostly remained together, being contained within an area of 4 or 5 square miles. Even so, the task of manoeuvring a large ship amongst the icefloes without crushing or overturning the small boats was extremely difficult and taxed Captain Rostron's skills to the limit. The painstaking task of recovering survivors took several hours and it was not until 8.00am that the last boat was located and brought alongside. This was number 12, which by now contained more than 70 people as survivors from the overturned collapsible B had been transferred to it as well as few from collapsible D. The last to come aboard the *Carpathia*, at 8.30am was the exhausted Second Officer Lightoller, now the senior surviving officer from the *Titanic*. It was none too soon as already the calm weather which had characterised the night was beginning to break and the sea was being whipped up by a freshening wind, making the rescue of the last survivors a difficult business. Rostron ordered the *Titanic*'s lifeboats to be hoisted aboard (13 were recovered in this way), and handed over the search for further survivors to Captain Lord in the *Californian* which had now arrived on the scene.

Before leaving the area, a brief but emotional service for those lost in the disaster was held in the *Carpathia*'s first class saloon as the ship passed over the spot where the *Titanic* was assumed to have sunk. By 8.50am the ship was underway, returning to New York to land the survivors, but it took the Cunard ship several hours to get free of the great icepack which had been the cause of the tragedy. The heart-rending task of counting and identifying the survivors then began, the eventual tally reaching 705 (201 first class, 118 second class and 179 third class passengers, together with 207 crew). While there is no doubt that Captain Rostron had saved all who were alive in the boats when he reached the area, it nevertheless began to dawn on all involved that more than twice this number, some 1,523 souls, must have perished when the ship went down. Most of the surviving passengers were women and their grief as they began to realise that they had lost their husbands or fathers or other relatives was heart-rending to see. The crew and passengers of the *Carpathia* rallied round to do what they could for all the survivors, regardless of their class or status.

One of the survivors was Bruce Ismay, the White Star Line chairman who, at Rostron's suggestion, composed a message to be sent to his company's offices in New York advising them of the sinking. It was dispatched in during the morning of the 15th and read,

TITANIC

"Deeply regret to advise you Titanic sank this morning after collision with iceberg, resulting in serious loss of life. Full particulars later, Ismay."

This was addressed to P. A. Franklin, the American vice president of IMM. Following on from this, preparations were made to transmit the long lists of survivors' names but the task proved too great for Cottam, the *Carpathia*'s radio operator, who had now been on continuous duty for over 24 hours and was on the point of collapse. Fortunately, one of the *Titanic*'s operators, Harold Bride, had been picked up and, although suffering from frostbite and exposure, he gamely volunteered to assist and was carried up to the radio

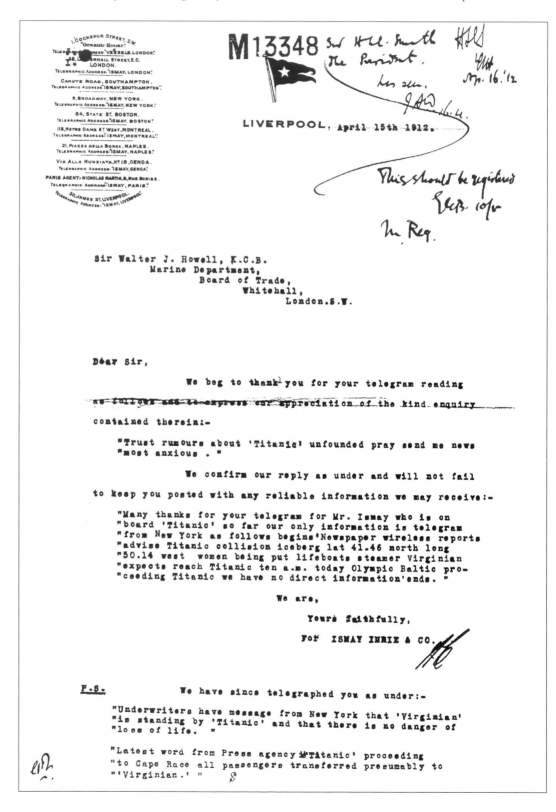

126

M14488

LIVERPOOL, April 16th, 1912.

Sir Walter J. Howell, K.C.B.
Marine Department, Board of Trade,
7, Whitehall Gardens,
London, S.W.

Dear Sir,

Further to our communication of yesterday we were extremely sorry to have to send you the following wire this morning :-

"Referring telegram yesterday 'Titanic' deeply grieved "say that during night we received word steamer foundered "about 675 souls mostly women and children saved".

which we now beg to confirm.

Yours faithfully,

For ISMAY. IMRIE & CO:

LEFT: A second communication from the White Star Line to the Board of Trade correcting the previous day's telegram and admitting to the dreadful news that *Titanic* had sunk with great loss of life.

BELOW: Thomas Pears was the 29-year old managing director of the Pears Soap Company. Married for just 18 months, he was travelling first class with his wife to look at a proposed new site for the company's first American venture. Tom Pears lost his life in the disaster.

room where he spent the rest of the voyage. It was another three days before the *Carpathia* arrived back at New York and berthed at Cunard's Pier 54 late in the evening of Thursday April 18, to be met by the American Press, eager to learn the details of the event about which little was known as Captain Rostron had not allowed transmission of any information other than the basic facts and the names of survivors.

As a footnote to this stage of the drama, it is pleasing to be able to record that the efforts of Captain Rostron and his crew were duly recognised. Even while still aboard the *Carpathia*, survivors from the *Titanic* organised a committee to raise a fund to express their gratitude and this later amounted to some $15,000. This was used to provide a distribution of cash to all members of the *Carpathia*'s crew and when the ship returned to New York some six weeks later, the opportunity was taken to present Captain Rostron with a specially commissioned silver loving cup while the crew all received specially struck commemorative medals. The management of the Cunard Line nobly refused to accept any payment for the services rendered by their ship and, indeed, added to the rewards bestowed on the crew by giving an extra month's wages to all who had been aboard at the time.

TITANIC

Union and employer relations at this time were not good and the *Titanic* disaster only made matters worse as this letter shows. At the heart of this is the indisputable fact that more people were rescued from first and second class than from the third class and crew. This is ascribed to class prejudice by Ben Tillett, one of the leaders of the Dock, Wharf, Riverside and General Workers' Union. He had organised the London Docks Strike of 1889.

M10619

Dock, Wharf, Riverside, and General Workers' Union
Of Great Britain and Ireland.

AFFILIATED WITH ...
"General Federation of Trades."
"International Federation (Transport.)"
"National Transport Workers' Federation."
"Trades Union Congress."
"Labour Party."

Telegraphic Address:
"DOCKERS, LONDON."
Telephone No. 1467 EAST.

General Secretary:
BEN TILLETT.

Registered Office:
425, MILE END ROAD,
LONDON, E.

Marine Dept

RESOLVED.

The Executive of the Dock, Wharf, Riverside & General Workers' Union hereby offers it's sincere condolences to the bereaved relatives of the Third Class passengers of the S/S "Titanic", whose tragic sinking we deplore. We also send our sincere regret to the relatives of the Crew, who were drowned. We also offer our strongest protest against the wanton and callous disregard of human life and the vicious class antagonism shown in the practical forbidding of the saving of the lives of the third class passengers. The refusal to permit other than the first class passengers to be saved by the boats, is in our opinion a disgrace to our common civilisation.

We therefore call upon the Government and the Board of Trade to insist on the provision of adequate life-saving appliances in boats. rafts and belts, which shall not only provide means of safety to the passengers, but to the whole members of the ship's staff.

We express our regret that in order to save time and cost, at the risk of life, shorter and quicker routes were insisted on, in spite of the knowledge of the presence of ice.

We trust the saving of so many first class passengers lives will not deaden the solicitude of the Government for the lives of those who belong to the wage earning classes, and call upon the members of the Labour Party to force upon the Government the necessity of proper protection to the lives of all mariners and all passengers, irrespective of class or grade.

Signed for the Executive.
BEN TILLETT.

The survivors of the *Titanic*'s crew were much less fortunate. For a start, the cash-strapped White Star Line stopped their wages from the moment that the ship sank. Although this was standard practice at the time, its application in these circumstances seemed particularly harsh. Most were transferred immediately to the *Lapland*, a ship belonging to the Red Star line, for the journey back to Plymouth, England. Four officers and over 30 other crew were subpoenaed to appear before an American committee of investigation, some actually being taken off the *Lapland* shortly after she had sailed.

As the news of the *Titanic*'s sinking slowly spread on both sides of the Atlantic there was shock and grief over the great loss of live, and bewilderment as to why such a tragedy could have happened. Then, as would happen today, there was intense public interest and speculation over the train of events, and an unconscious desire to find a scapegoat. At the same time the vested interests of maritime trade in general, and the White Star Line in particular, were less than pleased that some of their alleged shortcomings should be aired in public. There were to be two full scale inquiries, one in Britain held under the auspices of the Board of Trade and the other in America under the chairmanship of Senator William Smith. At first the British authorities resented any idea that the Americans had any right to carry out an inquiry as it concerned a British-registered ship, owned by a British Company, flying the British flag and manned by a British crew. However the Americans gave little credence to such niceties, pointing out the White Star Line was in fact itself owned by an American company and that many American citizens had died when the ship went down. Senator Smith was an energetic politician with an eye on the main chance and saw an opportunity to make a name for himself, to the extent that the official inquiry was conducted almost entirely by himself and in the full blaze of publicity, although nominally the committee included six other senators. To British eyes, the Americans were brash and erratic and did not know how to conduct a "formal" investigation. Be that as it may, the hearings, which took place between over 17 days between April 19 and May 25 in New York and Washington, elicited much significant information which was fresh in the minds of the many witnesses called. In fact there were no less than 82 witnesses, culled both from passengers and crew. The most significant witnesses were the ship's officers and some of the crew members, principally the lookouts and the radio operator. In addition Bruce Ismay was given a very hard time as Smith attempted to prove negligence on the part of IMM, the White Star Line's owners. Also of significance were the three witnesses from the *Californian*, including the Captain Lord who gave a factual account of the night's happenings from his point of view, while his fireman, Barrett, repeated his statement that he had seen a large ship and rockets being fired close to his own ship. In addition the radio operator, Cyril Evans, said that his captain had been informed three times about the rockets.

Edith Warne Pears, wife of Thomas was 22 years old. She was rescued in lifeboat No 8. Edith went on to drive ambulances during the First World War before her eventual remarriage.

The committee's final report and recommendations were published on May 28, 1912, only three days after the proceedings had ended. As well as setting out a narrative of the event, they also spotlighted the lack of lifeboat capacity together with the problems experienced in loading and lowering them. There was detailed discussion of the various wireless messages sent, and a considerable number of recommendations. These ranged widely from obvious improvements in the provision and equipping of lifeboats, through regulations to be applied to the manning and operation of maritime radio stations, to rules for the use of pyrotechnics at sea and substantial improvements in the design and construction of commercial vessels. The report also highlighted, in favourable terms, the actions of Captain Rostron and Senator Smith subsequently asked that legislation be enacted to allow the striking of a commemorative medal which would be presented to the captain by the President of the United States. However, the report also contained criticism of the way the lifeboats had been handled and loaded aboard the *Titanic* and of the professional conduct of Captain Smith who was held to have acted negligently in proceeding at speed through a known icefield, while the British government itself did not escape censure for failing to ensure that adequate provision was made for a potential disaster on this scale.

The results of the enquiry were naturally not received with pleasure in the United Kingdom, but one finding was eventually echoed and accepted at the subsequent British inquiry. This concerned Captain Lord of the *Californian* who was roundly condemned for his apparent inactivity on the night and was held to have been grossly negligent. It was strongly hinted that, if he had heeded what were assumed to have been unambiguous dis-

TITANIC

RIGHT: This question was put by Josiah Wedgwood, the Liberal MP for Newcastle-under-Lyme to the President of the Board of Trade. In it he asks why more children died in third class than in the rest of the ship. In fact all the children travelling in first and second were saved, while only 34.62 percent of children in third were spared from drowning.

FAR RIGHT: The death certificate for passengers travelling first class. In the first column is the date of the disaster April 15, 1912, the second column gives the place as about 41°16' Lat 50°14' Long. The third column starts the alphabetical list of passengers who died; the next gives their sex (almost exclusively men), the following completed column gives nationality, then address, and finally cause of death — unanimously drowning. A large number of wealthy and important people died, including John Jacob Astor, one of the wealthiest men in the world, Isidor Straus, the founder of Macy's department store and the designer of the Titanic, Thomas Andrews.

tress signals from the *Titanic*, his ship could have reached the scene before the liner sank and he could have rescued far more people than were actually in the lifeboats.

The British Board of Trade "Formal Investigation into the loss of the Steamship Titanic" began on May 2, 1912, while the American inquiry was still in progress. It was held, rather incongruously, in the drill hall of the London Scottish Regiment, not far from Buckingham Palace, and was under the direction of Lord Mersey, otherwise known as Mr. Justice Bingham, Baron Mersey of Toxteth (Lancashire). Other members of the board of inquiry, known as assessors, included experts in naval architecture and marine engineering, as well as professional seamen. The Board of Trade was represented by a formidable selec-

M11431
HOUSE OF COMMONS.

NOTICE given on *Thursday, 25th day of April* 1912

QUESTION to be put on *Monday, 29th day of April* 1912

36

Mr. Wedgwood, — To ask the President of the Board of Trade, whether the proposed British inquiry into the "Titanic" disaster will be able to inquire into the reason why the majority of the children in the steerage were drowned, while they were able to save those in the first and second class, and why the half-filled boats did not return to pick up the drowning as soon as the vessel sank. [*Monday 29th April.*]

Mr Buxton,-

As one of the principal objects of the investigation will be to ascertain the cause of the loss of life, I have no doubt that the points mentioned by my hon. friend will be dealt with by the Court of Inquiry.

NOTE. - It seems a pity to put questions of this kind.

TITANIC

To be filled in when an Official Log is not delivered.

MARRIAGES, BIRTHS, DEATHS AND INJURIES

that have occurred on board during the voyage.

	Date when married.	Christian and Surnames of both parties.	Age.	State whether Single, Widow or Widower.	Profession or Occupation.	Father's Christian and Surname.	Profession or Occupation of Father.
MARRIAGES.							

	Date of Birth.	Christian Name (if any) of Child.	Sex.	Christian Name and Surname of Father.	Rank, Profession or Occupation of Father.	Christian Name and Surname of Mother.	Maiden Surname of Mother.	Nationality and last place of abode. Father.	Nationality and last place of abode. Mother.	Signature of Father or Mother.	Signature of Master.
BIRTHS.											

FIRST CLASS PASSENGER DEPT

	Date. 1912	Place.	Christian Name and Surname of deceased.	Sex and Age.	Rank, Profession or Occupation.	Nationality (Stating Birthplace).	Last place of Abode.	Cause of Death. See footnotes.
					Members of Crew.		152 Abbey Rd. West Hampstead London N.W.	Drowning
1	April 15th	about	H. J. Allison	m				"
2	do.	41-16 Lat.	Mrs H. J. Allison	f.				"
3	do.	50-14 Long	Miss Allison	f.			Harland & Wolff Delfast	"
4	do.	do.	Thomas Andrews	m	Ship Builder	Irish	26 Rue Pasquier Paris	"
5	do.	do.	Ramon Artagaveytia	m				"
6	do.	do.	J J Astor	m		U.S.C	Hotel Ritz Paris	"
7			J. Baumann	m		U.S.C.	Grand Hotel — —	"
8			Quigg Baxter	m		U.S.C.	Elysee Palace Hotel Paris	"
9			T. Beattie	m		U.S.C.	Hotel Majestic, Nice	"
10			Stephen Weart Blackwell	m		U.S.C.		"
11			J J Borebank	m	Passengers.	Eng.		"
12			John B. Brady	m			Elysee Palace Hotel Paris	"
13			E. Brandeis	m				"
14			Arthur Jackson Brewe	m		U.S.C.		"
15			Archibald W. Butt	m		U.S.C.		"
16			Frank Carlson	m		U.S.C		"
17			J. M. Carran	m		U.S.C.		"
18			J. P. Carran	m				"

Under the heading "Cause of Death" should be entered, as fully as the space will allow, the chief circumstances attending the death.
If a fatal accident occurs at or about the time of any injury to the ship, or to any part of it, or to the cargo, the fact should be stated.
If a death occurs in port it should be stated whether it occurred on board or in hospital.
If a seaman dies on shore from an accident which happened or a disease which developed while he was a member of the crew, it is desirable that an entry of the death should be made in the same way.
As regards the account of wages and effects on form W. and E. 1 see note on the first page of this form.

	Date.	Place.	Name.	Rating on board.	Nature of Injury.	Circumstances.
INJURIES.	× see Nos 115					
				6/12	CA	

131

TITANIC

MARRIAGES, BIRTHS, DEATHS AND INJURIES

that have occurred on board during the voyage.

	Date when married.	Christian and Surnames of both parties.	Age.	State whether Single, Widow or Widower.	Profession or Occupation.	Father's Christian and Surname.	Profession or Occupation of Father.
MARRIAGES.							

	Date of Birth.	Christian Name (if any) of Child.	Sex.	Christian Name and Surname of Father.	Rank, Profession or Occupation of Father.	Christian Name and Surname of Mother.	Maiden Surname of Mother.	Nationality and last place of abode. Father.	Mother.	Signature of Father or Mother.	Signature of Master.
BIRTHS.											

(2ⁿᵈ class)

	Date. 1912	Place.	Christian Name and Surname of deceased.	Sex and Age.	Rank, Profession or Occupation.	Nationality (Stating Birthplace).	Last place of Abode.	address	Cause of Death. See footnotes.
124			Samson Abelson	M.	Members of Crew.	Russian	Paris		Drowning
125	April 15	About	Augustus C. Aldeworth	M.			London		"
126	do.	41.16. Lat	Edgar Andrew	M. 16			Southampton		"
127	do.	50.14. Long	Frank Andrew	M. 25	Miner	English	Redruth	"Fencoys" Four Lanes,	"
128	do.	do.	Wⁿ Argyle	M.		"	Warwick	14 Mill St. Warwick.	"
	do.		John Ashby	M. 57		U.S.A. citizen	London		"
	do.		Percy Bailey	M. 18	Butcher's Assist.	English	Penzance	25. Gwavas St.	"
131	do.		Chas. R. Bainbridge	M. 23	Horse Trainer Passengers.	"	Guernsey	Rohais Manor	"
132			Frederic J. Banfield	M. 28	Miner	"	Plymouth	30. Grenville Rd.	"
133	do.		Robet J. Bateman	M. 52			Soulton	Rudennis Road, Staple Hill Bristol	"
134	do.		Wⁿ Beauchamp	M.			London		"
135	do.		Wⁿ Berriman	M. 23	Miner		St. Ives	Hollesover St.	"

DEATHS.

Under the heading "Cause of Death" should be entered, as fully as the space will allow, the chief circumstances attending the death.
If a fatal accident occurs at or about the time of any injury to the ship, or to any part of it, or to the cargo, the fact should be stated.
If a death occurs in port it should be stated whether it occurred on board or in hospital.
If a seaman dies on shore from an accident which happened or a disease which developed while he was a member of the crew, it is desirable that an entry of the death should be made in the same way.
As regards the account of wages and effects on form W. and E. 1 see note on the first page of this form.

	Date.	Place.	Name.	Rating on board.	Nature of Injury.	Circumstances.
INJURIES.						

132

FAR LEFT: The death certificate for travellers in second class. The details are much the same as for first class, only this time some ages are given.

ABOVE LEFT: Percy Andrew Bailey (left) was apprenticed to a butcher in his home town of Penzance, Cornwall. Aged just 18, he had obtained a position in Akron, Ohio and purchased a second class ticket on the *Titanic*. Percy died in the disaster.

ABOVE: Edith Peacock (see caption page 135).

LEFT: Charles Joseph Shorney (back row, right) came from Sussex. Travelling third class, he was returning to his fiancée to open a taxi-cab company. Charles was taking much of his family's silverware with him, for which he hoped to get a better price than at home. Charles lost his life in the sinking.

TITANIC

MARRIAGES, BIRTHS, DEATHS AND INJURIES

that have occurred on board during the voyage.

	Date when married.	Christian and Surnames of both parties.	Age.	State whether Single, Widow or Widower.	Profession or Occupation.	Father's Christian and Surname.	Profession or Occupation of Father.
MARRIAGES.							

	Date of Birth.	Christian Name (if any) of Child.	Sex.	Christian Name and Surname of Father.	Rank, Profession or Occupation of Father.	Christian Name and Surname of Mother.	Maiden Surname of Mother.	Nationality and last place of abode. Father.	Mother.	Signature of Father or Mother.	Signature of Master.
BIRTHS.											

THIRD CLASS.

	Date. 1912	Place.	Christian Name and Surname of deceased.	Sex and Age.	Rank, Profession or Occupation.	Nationality (Stating Birthplace).	Last place of Abode.	Address	Cause of Death.
291	April 15	About	Mr Anthony Abbing	m 42	Blacksmith	U.S.A.	Southampton		Supposed Drowning
292	do.	44.16 Lat	Eugene Abbott	m. 13	Scholar	"	London	Salvation Army London	"
293	do.	50.14 Long	Rossmore Abbott	m. 16	Jeweller	"	"		"
294	do.	do.	Mauritis Adahl	m 30	Labourer	Sweden	Copenhagen		"
295	do.	do.	John Adams	m.	Farm Labr.	English	Yeovil	Hiatt Cottages Alum Chme Rd Bournemouth	"
296	do.	do.	Johanna Ahlin	F. 40.	Wife	Sweden	Gothenberg		"
297	do.	do.	Ali Ahmed	m. 24	Labr.	Syria	Buenos Ayres		"
298	do.	do.	William Alexander	m. 23	Labr.	England	Gt. Yarmouth	10. Belverdere Place Kitchener Rd Gt. Yarmouth	"
299	do.		Ilmari Alhomaki	m. 20	Labr.	Finland	Finland		"
300			William Ali	m. 25	Labr.	Syria	Buenos Ayres		"
301			William Allen	m. 35	Tool-maker	England	Birmingham	c/o F. Hunt 78. Queen's Rd Erdington	"
302			Owen George Allum	m. 18	Gardener	"	London	22. Oswald Rd. Southall	"
X 303			Anjos Saad	m 30	Farm Labr.	Syria	Syria		"
304			Albert Anderson	m. 33.	Engineer	Norway	Bergen.		"
305			Thor. Anderson	m. 20	Labr.	Norway	Christiana		"

Under the heading "Cause of Death" should be entered, as fully as the space will allow, the chief circumstances attending the death.
If a fatal accident occurs at or about the time of any injury to the ship, or to any part of it, or to the cargo, the fact should be stated.
If a death occurs in port it should be stated whether it occurred on board or in hospital.
If a seaman dies on shore from an accident which happened or a disease which developed while he was a member of the crew, it is desirable that an entry of the death should be made in the same way.
As regards the account of wages and effects on form W. and E. 1 see note on the first page of this form.

	Date.	Place.	Name.	Rating on board.	Nature of Injury.	Circumstances.
INJURIES.						
* see No 621			Aijo-Nirva			

134

tion of the legal profession led by the Attorney General himself, Sir Rufus Isaacs QC, while other legal worthies represented various interested parties including the White Star Line, the National Seamen's and Firemen's Union, the *Californian*'s owners and crew, and the passengers. Sir Cosmo and Lady Duff-Gordon had their own legal representatives. The inquiry took the form of 26 questions presented by Sir Rufus Isaacs, to which the proceedings would attempt to establish answers. Most of these covered predictable matter such as the design and construction of the vessels, the events leading up to the tragedy and the aftermath of the sinking. The most controversial question turned out to be Number 24 which, as originally framed, read as follows.

"What was the cause of the loss of the *Titanic* and of the loss of lives which thereby ensured or occurred? Was the construction of the vessel and its arrangement such as to make it difficult for any class of passenger or any portion of the crew to take full advantage of the existing provisions for safety?"

This question, or rather two as written, was loaded enough with implications and innuendo but during the course of the inquiry was altered at the instigation of the Attorney General by the insertion of a further query which read,

"What vessels had the opportunity of rendering assistance to the *Titanic*, and, if any, how was it that assistance did not reach the *Titanic* before the steamship *Carpathia* arrived."

This was squarely aimed at the wretched Captain Lord who was grilled at some length by the Attorney General while the somewhat conflicting evidence of other officers and crew members was to be selectively handled in the final report.

However Lord was not the only person who caused more than usual public interest in what otherwise became a lengthy, technical, and, ultimately, rather boring affair. The occupants of lifeboat number 1 had included the wealthy Sir Cosmo Duff-Gordon and his society wife and fashion entrepreneur Lady Lucy Duff-Gordon. On the fifth day of the proceedings, Leading Fireman Charles Hendrickson, who had been assigned to this boat, stated that he had wanted to go back and rescue screaming survivors in the water but that the Duff-Gordons had prevented him, even though the boat was less than half full. He also confirmed that he and the other crew members in the boat had each received a cheque £5 each from Sir Cosmo before the *Carpathia* reached New York. Subsequently no less than one and of half days of the inquiry's (expensive) time was spent going into to every nuance of this little drama and Sir Cosmo himself was called to give his account, which was basically that he had given the money in recognition that the seaman had lost everything and out of sheer gratitude for surviving. He denied that he or his wife had obstructed any attempt to rescue other survivors, but admitted that no such attempt had actually been made. Much of London's polite society turned out to see how the Duff-Gordons would fare, but otherwise public interest waned as the inquiry dragged on.

Not that there was a shortage of interesting witnesses although, unlike the American hearing, no passengers were called to give evidence. The surviving ship's officers, Lightoller, Pitman, Boxhall and Lowe, were all put through the mill with Lightoller himself answering no fewer than 1,600 questions! Ismay and Sanderson, White Star Line directors, did their best to convince the inquiry that the *Titanic* complied with all regulations and that the former had not influenced Captain Smith's actions in any way. Independent witnesses included the noted explorer, Sir Ernest Shackleton, who gave his expert opinion on the characteristics of icepacks and icebergs and an assessment of how likely it was that a particular ice-floe would be seen under various conditions. The closing days of the hearing were occupied with the testimony of various technical witnesses, including some significant statements from respected mariners who confirmed

LEFT: The death certificate for travellers in third class. Note the number of Scandinavians; 62 percent of third class passengers were drowned while 62 percent of first class passengers were saved.

BELOW: Originally from Carnkie in Cornwall, Edith Nile Peacock booked third class tickets for herself, three-year old daughter, Treasteall, and seven-month old baby, Alfred. Her husband, Benjamin, was never even to see his new son, as Edith and both children lost their lives.

that it was not accepted practice at the time for ships to slow down when ice was known to be in the vicinity. After the last witness had appeared on June 21, 1912, a further eight days were occupied with submissions and statements by counsels for the various interested parties and it was not until July 3, after 36 arduous working days, that the official enquiry was ended.

Lord Mersey presented his final report on July 30 and it contained no surprises. In fact, considering the nature and scale of the tragedy, it was remarkably restrained. It found that the basic cause was that the *Titanic* was being navigated at excessive speed in view of the conditions but, nevertheless, did not find Captain Smith to have been negligent in this respect. There was criticism of the arrangements for manning the lifeboats and the Board

A letter sent by Sir Edward Grey from the British Embassy in Washington to London reporting on the findings of the Senate Committee into the *Titanic* disaster. The head of the investigation was William Alden Smith, Senator for Michigan, he was empowered to look into the matter despite *Titanic* being a British ship, because the White Star Line was owned by an American trust, the International Mercantile Marine Co. This in turn meant that they could be sued under American law, if negligence could be proved. Senator Smith's motives are questionable but he did point the finger of blame at the Board of Trade inspector for hurrying his inspection during *Titanic*'s trials, at Captain Smith for ignoring the presence of ice on her route, to the actions of the captain of the *Californian*, and the inadequate number, boarding and launching of the lifeboats. The letter quotes the final remarks that Senator Smith would make in his speech to the Senate on the disaster, ". . .we shall leave to the honest judgement of England its painstaking chastisement of the Board of Trade to whose laxity of regulation and hasty inspection the world is largely indebted for this awful fatality."

NO. *153*   M16719 BRITISH EMBASSY 23700

WASHINGTON 4 JUN 1912
May 27, 1912.

Sir,

　　With reference to previous correspondence I have the honour to inform you that the report of the Senate Committee of investigation into the "Titanic" disaster will be published to-morrow at midday.　Although I have been unable to procure copies of this report in time to despatch them by this mail, I have been permitted to see a revise of the report of the Committee.　It is understood that Mr. Smith, the President of the Committee, had desired to make the report somewhat more denunciatory but was eventually over-ruled by his colleagues. The report, which on the whole may be said to be couched in moderate terms, attacks with some vehemence the action of the Commander of the "Californian" and lays considerable stress on the small heed that was given to the warnings of the presence of ice in the track of the "Titanic", while the method of filling and launching ~~and launching~~ the lifeboats is also censured. It further condemns the hasty inspection of the vessel by the Board of Trade Inspector during her trials.　As regards the suggestions for safeguarding life, the report states that the United States accepts on the reciprocal basis the inspection certificate of foreign countries, but that unless foreign countries speedily revise their inspection laws on the lines laid down in the report "the Committee deems it proper that such reciprocal arrangements be terminated". The lines laid down

are

The Right Honourable,
　　Sir Edward Grey, Bart., K.G.,
　　　　etc., etc., etc.,

'TITANIC" DISASTER

HEARING

BEFORE A

SUBCOMMITTEE OF THE COMMITTEE ON COMMERCE UNITED STATES SENATE

SIXTY-SECOND CONGRESS

SECOND SESSION

PURSUANT TO

S. RES. 283

DIRECTING THE COMMITTEE ON COMMERCE TO INVES-
TIGATE THE CAUSES LEADING TO THE WRECK
OF THE WHITE STAR LINER "TITANIC"

PART 15

DIGEST OF TESTIMONY

Printed for the use of the Committee on Commerce

WASHINGTON
GOVERNMENT PRINTING OFFICE
1912

Six senators under the chairmanship of Senator William Alden Smith produced a huge report on the disaster. This is the digest of the testimonies heard by the Subcommittee of the Committee on Commerce United States Senate.

of Trade was castigated for not ensuring that its regulations had kept pace with technolog-ical progress. Both Bruce Ismay and Sir Cosmo Duff-Gordon were found not have acted improperly and, once again, Captain Rostron of the *Carpathia* was praised for his actions. Although the inquiry was by no means a court of law, it effectively found Captain Lord of the *Californian* guilty of gross negligence and implied that he was directly responsible for the loss of the many souls which it was alleged he could have rescued.

And that was that!

RETROSPECT

TITANIC

The landing of the Titanic's survivors in New York, and the ensuing American and British hearings were by no means the end of the story. In fact they were merely the opening pages in a story which has steadfastly refused to die and has become part of twentieth century legend, with fact and fiction so completely intertwined that it is difficult to tell one from the other. As the scale of the tragedy became apparent, moving and grief-ridden memorial services were held in New York, St. Paul's Cathedral in London and at Belfast. Perhaps the most poignant was at St. Mary's church in Southampton, only a short distance from the berth in Southampton docks from whence the *Titanic* had set off on its ill-fated voyage. The town was devastated as many of the 700 crew lost when the ship went down had their homes and families in the area. In order to raise money for them, and for the families of the 800 passengers also lost, fund-raising concerts, performances and other events were held not only in the United Kingdom and America, but in Canada, New Zealand, Australia and many other parts of the world which had been affected in some way or other. On both sides of the Atlantic memorials were erected to honour those who died and fittingly, among the very first of these were examples at Liverpool, Boston and New York dedicated to the brave musicians who kept playing until the very end and who perished to a man.

The end of the official inquiries did not mark the end of legal activity. Indeed it was only the start as companies and individuals sought damages and compensation from the White Star Line for the loss of relatives, goods, and cargo. They had, of necessity, awaited the outcome of the official inquiries before proceeding with their own cases: had the White Star Line or its servants or agents been found plainly negligent in the discharge of their responsibilities, then the way would have been clear for all concerned to press ahead with their claims for massive damages. As it was, neither inquiry made a clear-cut assignment of responsibility and it therefore appeared unlikely that claimants in the United Kingdom would receive anything beyond the meagre allowances under the Merchant Shipping Act. In America, several major claims were filed and these were considered by the Southern District Court for the State of New York, the total involved being in the region of almost $17 million. The White Star Line contested these claims and brought a counter suit to American courts in which it sought to limit its liabilities to the salvage value of the *Titanic*'s assets, as permitted under American law. These consisted of the value of the 13 lifeboats recovered by the *Carpathia*, together with pre-paid freight charges and revenue from passenger tickets, which together came to $97,772. However it was eventually ruled that British law would stand in this instance and battle between the legal representatives of the claimants and those of White Star intensified. The hearing of these cases dragged on for some time, and probably would have continued for longer had it not been for the outbreak of the First World War which forced attention on other issues. In the end the lawyers for the various parties agreed on a settlement under which the sum of $663,000 was paid to the claimants, to be distributed on a pro rata basis, and the proceedings were formally closed on July 28, 1916.

Whilst the arguments raged ashore, the wreck of the *Titanic* lay at a depth of 12,500ft in the middle of the Atlantic Ocean. Tentative plans to salvage the ship were laid in the immediate aftermath but these came to naught and, given the technology of the time, had little chance of success. With the outbreak of war in August 1914, the *Titanic* story began to fade from prominence as other great ships became victims of the conflict. The most famous of these was the *Lusitania*, sunk off the Irish coast by a German U-boat on May 7, 1915, with great loss of life, while the *Titanic*'s sister ship, the *Britannic*, was lost in the Mediterranean in November 1916 when serving as a hospital ship. When the lives lost in these and hundreds of other sinkings was added to the millions killed in the Armaggedon of the fighting on land, the scale of the *Titanic*'s losses, perhaps understandably, began to fade in public memory, although, of course, not in the thoughts of the families of those directly affected. In the years between the wars, people generally did not have the time, money or technology to attempt any salvage of the vessel although this did not stop exag-

gerated rumours of great treasures buried within the wreck, this being enough to cause a few hopefuls to come forward with wildly impractical schemes.

War broke out again in 1939, causing many more fine ships to be sent to the bottom before peace reigned again in 1945 and by the early 1950s there was a definite reawakening of interest in the *Titanic* and the possibility of locating and salvaging at least part of the wreck. One UK salvage company, Rosdon Beasley Ltd, actually spent a week in the vicinity of the sinking using a technique of recording sound waves from undersea explosions in an unsuccessful attempt to locate the wreck. In 1955 public attention was aroused by a best selling account of the sinking entitled *A Night to Remember* written by Walter Lord. Of course there were many other books on the same subject published at various times right up to the present day, but Lord's treatment of the events of that night was written in a dramatic style which caught the imagination; it was subsequently made into a highly successful film. That the *Titanic* still provides an endless source of fascination is illustrated by the fact that a current front rank novelist, Beryl Bainbridge, has made the sinking the centre of a book written as recently as 1996.

In the meantime, schemes to locate the wreck began to proliferate following the postwar success of underwater exploration methods and the development during the cold war period of high frequency scanning sonars, which give very detailed images of the seabed. By the late 1970s a number of groups had been set up, including an alliance between Walt Disney Productions and the *National Geographic* magazine which was intended to produce a film based on the story of the sinking and the subsequent rediscovery of the wreck. In Britain, there was Seawise & Titanic Salvage Ltd, a company financed by Sir James Goldsmith (he of the current Referendum Party), which deployed considerable technical expertise but its expedition planned for the summer of 1980 did not come to fruition. It was left to an American millionaire, Jack Grimm, to make the first realistic attempts to find the *Titanic* during the course of no fewer than three expeditions in the early 1980s. In July and August 1980, he teamed up with scientists from the Scripps Institute of Oceanography in California and the Lamont-Doherty Geological Observatory, part of the New York's Columbia University, and searched an area in mid-Atlantic aboard the research ship

TITANIC

RIGHT: Michael Navratil's grave in Halifax, Nova Scotia.

BELOW: Mount Olive Cemetery, Halifax, Nova Scotia.

H. J. W. Fay. Altogether 14 potential targets were located, but none were positively identified as being the actual wreck. In the following year he spent another 10 days aboard the research vessel *Gyre* searching an area slightly south of that covered in the previous year but then, as before, he was bedevilled by bad weather. However, in the very last sweep a prototype undersea video system was deployed and it was only when the signals were being decoded whilst on the voyage home that an object swam into view which Grimm subsequently claimed was undoubtedly one of the *Titanic's* propellers. However, none of the scientists who accompanied him were prepared to substantiate this claim, and a subsequent Grimm expedition in 1983 failed to add anything further to the search.

In the meantime the Scripps Institute co-operated with the Massachusett's Woods Hole Oceanographic Institute to carry out a preliminary expedition in 1981 under the auspices of the US Office of Naval Research, although this was more a test of new equipment than a serious attempt to find the *Titanic*. In 1985 the Woods Hole Institute teamed up with the Institute Français de Recherches pour l'Exploitation des Mers (IFREMER — the French Institute for Research and Exploitation of the Seas) to launch an expedition under the joint leadership of Dr. Robert Ballard and Jean-Louis Michel from the US and French institutes respectively. The first stage of the search was carried out between July 9 and August 7 by the French vessel *Le Suroît* using a deep towed sideways scanning high resolution sonar which swept 1,000-yard wide swathes as it was towed backwards and forwards across the designated search area. This area had been carefully planned and took into account the results of Grimm's searches together with a calculation of all the factors which might have affected the accuracy of Boxhall's calculations on the night of the sinking. Consequently the *Le Suroît* concentrated on an area covering 150 square miles mainly to the south and east of 41°46'N and 50°14'W, the position which the fourth officer had plotted at the time. Again bad weather intervened and nothing was found by the time that the vessel had to depart, being needed for tasks elsewhere.

The second phase of the operation began on August 22 when the US Navy research vessel *Knoor* arrived to carry on the search with Ballard and Michel aboard, these scientists having transferred from the French ship. The main American equipment was a towed platform called *Argo* which carried not only forward-looking and sideways-scanning sonar, but also some highly sophisticated real time video cameras which could transmit high quality images via an optic fibre link to the control cabin aboard the ship. The first task was to investigate the sonar targets and "propeller" located by the Grimm expeditions and all these were quickly eliminated from the search which then moved to the areas not already covered by the French activity. For days on end *Argo* was towed back and forth across the Atlantic seabed until, as the operating team struggled to stay awake in the early hours of September 1, a number of obviously man-made objects suddenly started to appear on their screens. This was immediately followed by a shout from the sonar operator that he had a contact ahead of the *Argo*. The ship's cook was sent to fetch Robert Ballard who rushed into the control room just after large round object had swum into view — it was a the face of a ship's boiler! As the control room erupted into whoops and cheers of celebration, Ballard had the presence of mind to order the *Argo* to be raised a 100ft or so away from the seabed in order to prevent it being damaged or lost by actually hitting the side of the *Titanic's* great hull. As the *Knoor* paused after the initial pass over the newly found wreck, realisation dawned that it was now nearly 2.00am, almost to the hour the time that the *Titanic* had gone down. A sombre mood broke into the celebrations and, led by Ballard, many of the crew went and stood silently on the quarterdeck, lost in thoughts of what had happened in that very spot over 73 years earlier. Then it was back to work — the *Titanic* had been found at last!

Time was now short, as the *Knoor* could only remain on station for a few more days and operations were affected by worsening weather which made the launch and retrieval of the *Argo* a dangerous business. Nevertheless, several more runs were made over the wreck, many at really close quarters passing only a few feet above the wreck. It was established that the ship lay upright although all four funnel had collapsed and it appeared that the hull had broken into two separate sections, the break occurring in the region of the third funnel. The forward section was reasonably intact although there was some damage to the forward port side caused when the ship hit the bottom, the foremast had collapsed across the bow and there was a large hole where the forefunnel had fallen away as the ship bow plunged under the surface. Although good quality images of the whole forward section were obtained, there was not enough time to survey the stern section before the *Knoor* set course for home on the morning September 4, 1984. Nevertheless the expedition had been a resounding success, with news of the achievement leaking out even as the *Knoor* sailed for home. In fact none of the scientists, or their parent organisations, had foreseen the tremendous media interest which the finding of the *Titanic* would release and they were surprised to find helicopters flying out to the ship in order to gather copies of films and video tapes for transmission across the world. When the *Knoor* eventually reached Wood's Hole on September 9, it was met by an umbrella of aircraft and helicopters, while the normally quiet haven was filed with sightseeing and official craft. The dockside was covered with cheering crowds and news cameras, aerials and satellite dishes littered the whole area.

As the scientists stepped ashore, they were taken immediately to a massive press conference where they briefly told of the great team effort and leading edge technology which had made the discovery possible. Other media occasions followed and later, in Washington DC, Dr. Ballard ended one of these proceedings with a the following thoughtful statement.

"The *Titanic* itself lies in 13,000ft of water on a gently sloping alpine like countryside overlooking a small canyon below. Its bow faces north and the ship sits upright on the bottom. Its mighty stacks point upward.

"There is no light at this great depth and little light can be found. It is quiet and peaceful and a fitting place for the remains of this greatest of sea tragedies to rest.

"May it forever remain that way and may God bless these found souls".

Unfortunately these well expressed noble sentiments would be almost impossible to apply, as the very finding of the wreck had thrown the whole story of the *Titanic* firmly into the public eye and several individuals came forward with schemes to raise the ship or at least to salvage major sections with the idea of using them for commercial museums and other schemes. In an effort to prevent random and possibly damaging salvage attempts on the hull, the United States enacted legislation in 1986 in the form of the *Titanic* Memorial Act, although whether this had any standing in international law was open to debate.

In 1986 Ballard led a further expedition to the now precisely known location of the wreck but this time it was an all-American effort due to a disagreement with IFREMER over the film and video rights from the previous year. A new research vessel, *Atlantis II*, was made available and the towed *Argo* platform was replaced by a three-man deep-diving submersible belonging to the US Navy, *Alvin* which substantially funded the expedition as a means of testing various undersea equipment and techniques in a project which pushed out the boundaries of achievement in this field. *Alvin* had been adapted to carry a small self-propelled camera-equipped device named *Jason Junior* (*JJ*) which was powered and controlled through a 250ft long umbilical cable linking it to the submersible. This carried high definition video and film cameras, as well as the necessary lighting system, and using this combination it would be possible for scientists to see the wreck at first hand, while *JJ* could actually be manouvred inside the hull to visit cabins, passageways and machinery spaces. If it worked, the results would be fascinating and there was an air of eager anticipation as the first dive was made on July 13, 1986.

This time the weather was kind and sea conditions were calm. As the wreck had been accurately pinpointed the previous year, *Alvin* was able to be steered directly towards it but, as it came into sight, the dive had to be abandoned due to a technical fault. A second dive was more successful but an unexpectedly strong current caused the planned initial deployed of *JJ* on the third dive to be cancelled. However the fourth dive was completely successful and *JJ* was steered through the great hole left by the missing forefunnel and passed down

Millvina Dean was the youngest *Titanic* survivor — she was just nine weeks old — at the time of the tragedy. She is seen here with her mother and brother, Bertram Vere Dean.

TITANIC

Titanic survivors Eva Hart, Millvina Dean and Edith Haisman at the British *Titanic* Society's convention in 1995.

into B deck, allowing the first views inside the ship for 74 years. The scientists had been apprehensive at the possibility of coming across gruesome human remains but in the event none were seen, time and the sea having completely erased any traces although items of clothing were often found in positions where their wearers had died. Over the next few dives the team became more confident as the gained experience and explored the Boat Deck, the crow's nest, the bridge, and even went into the purser's office, tugging at the safe handle to see if it would open (it didn't!). Almost threequarters of a mile behind the bow section was a field of debris which had been carried away by the current as the doomed ship broke up and sank to the bottom. On one dive *Alvin* and *JJ* roamed over this area where thousands of artifacts such as plates, crockery, pots, pans, heaters, and other cabin fittings could be plainly seen, as could huge piles of coal shed from the ship's bunkers.

Dive eight concentrated on the stern section which lay about 600 yards behind the bow section and was in much worse shape, most of the decks having collapsed onto each other as this section hit the bottom with some force. In other dives some attempt was made to view the damage caused by the collision with the iceberg but this part of the hull was completely buried and could not be seen. In all, *Alvin* made 11 manned dives, completing its programme on July 24, 1986 when *Atlantis II* then set cause back to Wood's Hole, arriving home on July 28. The extraordinary pictures obtained by this expedition were again made available for television viewing, and also featured in several books, notably Ballard's own account of the expeditions which was first published in 1987.

While Ballard was painstaking in ensuring that nothing aboard the *Titanic* was disturbed or retrieved, his erstwhile French colleagues were less scrupulous and the oil millionaire Jack Grimm negotiated a joint expedition with IFREMER with the intention of recovering artifacts from the wreck. In the event Grimm was not involved in the final consortium which married several American business interests with IFREMER and other French agencies. Reaching the area of the *Titanic* wreck on July 22, 1987 aboard the support vessel *Nadir*, the American-backed French team used equipment very similar to that used by Ballard the year before. This consisted of the manned submersible *Nautile* which

In the High Court of Justice

KING'S BENCH DIVISION.

SUPREME COURT OF JUDICATURE / 30 JUN.1913 / CENTRAL OFFICE / WRIT. APPEAR. JUDGT.

1912 , ℛ , No. 1111

BETWEEN

Thomas Ryan

Plaintiff,

—— AND ——

Oceanic Steam Navigation Company Limited

Defendants

I CERTIFY that this action was tried before The *Honourable Mr Justice Bailhache*

and a *Special* Jury of the County of Middlesex,

on the 20th, 23rd 24th, 25th & 26th days of *June* 1913 .

On the question of negligence

THE JURY FOUND *answers to the following questions :—*

1. *Was the navigation of the Titanic negligent in respect of (A) look out ? Ans: No (B) Speed ? Ans: Yes.*

2. *Was the marconigram from the Mesaba communicated in due course to some responsible officer of the Titanic ? Ans: Not evidence sufficient.*

On the question of contract the jury found answers to the ~~The Jury returned and answered with a verdict in the~~ *following question:*

1. *Did the Defendants do what was reasonably sufficient to give Moran notice of the conditions having regard to Moran's condition in life ? Ans: No.*

2. *Did the Defendants do what was reasonably sufficient to give Ryan notice of the conditions having regard to Ryan's condition in life ? Ans: No:*

and by consent assessed the damages at £100 =

The Judge directed that Judgment should be entered

(22,225). Wt.34,764—1440. 2500. 3/10. A.&E.W.

(over)

The writ between Thomas Ryan and The Oceanic Steam Navigation Co Ltd. The particulars of the negligence were:

". . .that they navigated the said Ship at an excessive speed and at an improper speed in view of the conditions then prevailing namely the exceptional darkness of the night the hazy condition of the atmosphere the absence of wind and movement of the sea at and immediately preceeding the time of the collision and of the presence of icebergs and fields of ice in the course of the said vessel: that while knowing of the presence of the said field they failed to alter their course or to diminish their speed so as to avoid the same and failed to provide a sufficient and proper look-out therefor and to supply look-out men with Binoculars: that no adequate lifeboat accommodation was provided on the said Ship having regard to the number of passengers and crew she was then carrying: and that the Defendants failed to have the said crew sufficiently drilled and organized for the work of manning filling and launching such lifeboats as were provided . . ."

---

deployed *Robin*, a remotely operated mechanical probe. During a period of just over seven weeks, the team made no less than 32 dives and recovered around 1,800 objects which ranged from small items such as plates, to many of the ship's fittings including masthead lights, a telegraph from the bridge, and much more. Many of these items were exhibited in Paris and subsequently part of the collection toured Scandinavia in 1991 and 1992 (many of the families travelling on the *Titanic* had originated from this part of the world; as an 'emigrant' ship, she was carrying many people to a new life in the New World).

Now that the precise location of the *Titanic* was known, it became a magnet for other

TITANIC

Writ issued the 3rd day of July 1912.

BETWEEN   THOMAS Ryan   Plaintiff

and

THE OCEANIC STEAM NAVIGATION

COMPANY LIMITED   Defendants.

_____

S T A T E M E N T   of   C L A I M.

    The Plaintiff brings this action for the benefit of him-
self the father of Patrick Ryan deceased he having suffered damage
from the Defendants' negligence in carrying the said Patrick Ryan
on their Steamship "Titanic" on a voyage from Queenstown to New
York hereby the said Patrick Ryan was drowned in consequence of
the said ship colliding with an Iceberg and foundering in the
North Atlantic Ocean on the 15th April 1912.

<u>Particulars of negligence.</u>

The negligence of the Defendants servants consisted
in this that they navigated the said Ship at an excessive speed and at an improper speed in view of the conditions then prevailing namely the exceptional darkness
of the night the hazy condition of the atmosphere the
absence of wind and movement of the sea at and immediately preceding the time of the collision and of the
presence of icebergs and fields of ice in the course of
the said vessel: that while knowing of the presence of
the said ice they failed to alter their course or to
diminish their speed so as to avoid the same and failed
to provide a sufficient and proper look-out therefor and
to supply look-out men with Binoculars: that no adequate
lifeboat accommodation was provided on the said Ship

exploration groups eager to test their capabilities and technology on one of the famous shipwrecks of all time. 1991 a film company made a series of dives using equipment chartered from Russian sources. Using the high quality IMAX® process intended for projection on to wide, wraparound, screens giving audiences a sense of participation in the events they were seeing, a series of absolutely stunning images were obtained and made into a feature film entitled *Titanica*. In 1992 a company called Marex-*Titanic* Inc., backed yet again by Jack Grimm among others, raised an expedition which sailed at the end of the year but by the time its vessel, *Sea Mussel*, had reached the site, the company was deeply embroiled in legal arguments which eventually forced it to withdraw without ever diving on the wreck. Their protagonists were *Titanic* Ventures which had been a partner in the successful Franco-American foray in 1987 and laid claim to the "salvor in possession", a legal term which if sustained would mean that they had sole rights to the removal of any artifacts from the wreck. The legal wrangle dragged on until the end of 1993 when *Titanic* Ventures, now known as RMS *Titanic* Inc., was finally granted the legal right to work on the wreck and some further dives were made in 1993 and 1994 to recover more material. A small but significant part of the collection gathered over the years featured in a major exhibition at Britain's National Maritime Museum at Greenwich, this display opening on October 4, 1994 and official guests included a number of survivors of the sinking. When the exhibition finally closed in April 1995, almost threequarters of a million people had been drawn to come and learn the story of the *Titanic* and to view the fascinating collection of pieces drawn up at such great expense from the bottom of the ocean. When it ended, two *Titanic* survivors, Edith Haisman and Eva Hart, joined in a ceremony to dedicate a memorial to the victims of the disaster in the grounds of the museum. Surprisingly this was the first public memorial to the *Titanic* to be erected in London. RMS *Titanic* Inc. are currently involved in a scheme to mount a permanent *Titanic* display aboard a barge which could then be towed to ports around the world, enabling even more access to one of the world's greatest dramas.

It is perhaps fitting that permanent exhibition will be available for generations to come, because the numbers of those able to recount first-hand experiences of the sinking are dwindling fast. Of the ship's officers, the captain, chief and first officers all perished. Of the surviving officers, the longest lived was Fourth Officer Boxhall, who died in 1967 and at one time acted as technical advisor in the making of the film *A Night to Remember*. Bruce Ismay, the White Star Line chairman who was pilloried by the American press as "Brute" Ismay, relinquished his post shortly after the sinking although remaining as an IMM executive until 1916. He continued to be active in other companies until his retirement in 1934 and died in October 1937, aged 74. Few surviving passengers and crew remain, their numbers now shrinking rapidly as time takes its toll. One person who became intimately bound up with the affair, although not aboard the *Titanic*, was Captain Lord of the *Californian*. Despite the facts available to them, both inquiries had made up their minds that he could have done more to assist the sinking ship. Although Lord started legal action to clear his name, the advent of the First World War caused him to put the matter aside and he took no further action, continueing an otherwise unblemished career at sea until he retired in 1927. Although he died in 1967, he had several supporters who petitioned the Board of Trade to reconsider the case, all to no avail. However the locating of the *Titanic*'s wreck in 1985 some miles from the originally presumed position of the sinking provided enough "new evidence" to cause the Secretary of State for Transport to commission a review of the all the evidence by officials of the Marine Accident Investigation Branch in 1990 but the resulting report, which was not fully accepted by independent observers, did not do much to restore Lord's good name although it questioned the actions of his second officer who, it was felt, had not done enough to inform his captain of the various sightings of rockets during the night. Nevertheless, the report did come to the conclusion that any actions Captain Lord might reasonably have been expected to carry out, would not have made any difference to the outcome of the sinking, or to the number of survivors rescued.

Statement of Claim
The scramble to deny responsibility for the loss of the *Titanic* was carried out at the highest levels in both London and Washington, at the end of which no general compensation was paid out. Tickets issued by the White Star Line for *Titanic* were not in line with Board of Trade requirements but they still held good in the courts. On the back each ticket stated that the owners would not be liable for any loss or damage caused by the negligent navigation of the vessel by the company or its servants.

This is the written judgement on the claim brought in the High Court of Justice between Thomas Ryan the father of a victim and the Oceanic Steam Navigation Co Ltd (otherwise known as the White Star Line). Patrick Ryan and James Moran both drowned in the disaster and their families united to sue the owners for negligence based on the findings of the Commission of Enquiry. The judge awarded in favour of the plaintiffs. The company appealed but the verdict was upheld.

TITANIC

The question that was in everybody's mind at the time and still remains unanswered today is why the tragedy occurred at all. In modern times it is inconceivable that it would happen given the accuracy of modern electronic navigation equipment, a system of warnings by radio and satellite transmissions and the incalculable contribution of radar. Modern safety standards would ensure that, even if collision took place, there would be far less chance of a large ship actually sinking and, in any case, there would be adequate lifesaving equipment available, not to mention the intervention of aircraft and helicopters. But, of course, none of this was available to the *Titanic* and her crew. Despite the tremendous increase in the size and speed of merchant ships, navigation was still carried out by methods which had been perfected in the era of Captain Cook and had changed little since. Radar was non-existent and the locating of vessels and other objects could only by visual means, even at night. Despite this, sea travel appeared to be extremely safe and at the British inquiry the point was made that in the previous 20 years there had been an estimated 32,000 Atlantic crossings in which a total of only 148 people had died as a result of marine accidents.

To modern eyes, Captain Smith must appear criminally negligent as he drove his ship at over 20kts into an area known to be littered with icebergs and yet, by the standards of his day, this was acceptable and normal practice, as was testified at the hearings. More to the point, there is absolutely no evidence that any of the other officers aboard the ship even thought of suggesting to the captain that it would be wise to slow down. There was perhaps an unspoken assumption that because no large liner on the Atlantic run had ever hit an iceberg, then it would never happen in the future. This might seem incredible, but similar patterns of thinking have been shown to be a common factor in accidents at sea, on land or in the air, right up to the present. The loss of the *Herald of Free Enterprise* off Zeebrugge in 1987 occurred because, although the roll-on roll-off ferry concept was known to carry inherent risks if the vehicle deck became flooded, it was assumed that this could never happen. In the case of the *Titanic*, the sheer size and apparent strength of the ship gave great confidence to those associated with her, and while she was not unsinkable from a purely technical point of view, it seemed inconceivable that she could suffer so much damage in any collision that she would not float. Thus the captain and crew were obviously quite satisfied in their own minds that they would see any ice in their path in good time to slow down or avoid it, and that even if they should be so unfortunate as to strike an iceberg it would not cause serious damage. Both of these assumptions were to be cruelly undermined but until midnight on April 14, 1912, few people would have thought otherwise.

One other point of hindsight was raised at the British inquiry. The prompt and totally correct actions of First Officer Murdoch on being told of the iceberg ahead have already been recounted. However one of Harland & Wolff's naval architects, Edward Wilding, revealed under questioning that if the *Titanic* had maintained its course and speed and hit the iceberg head on, she would not have sunk although there would have been considerable damage to the bow section and around 200 casualties, mostly amongst crew members and third class passengers accommodated in that part of the ship. Of course, nobody seriously suggested that Murdoch should have acted other than he did but, if the lookouts had not sighted the iceberg until a few seconds later it might have changed the outcome.

With regular publication of films and books on the subject, there is little doubt that the drama of the *Titanic* will continue to weave a powerful spell for generations to come. The ship itself is gradually deteriorating and by the middle of the twenty-first century may no longer be a recognisable shape on the seabed, but the image of the great liner sinking slowly into the sea on that starry April night with its lights blazing and the band playing will be forever etched on the face of maritime history, and the whole scene will be instantly replayed in people's minds by the mention of a single word — *Titanic.*

TITANIC

Scene from *Raise the Titanic*

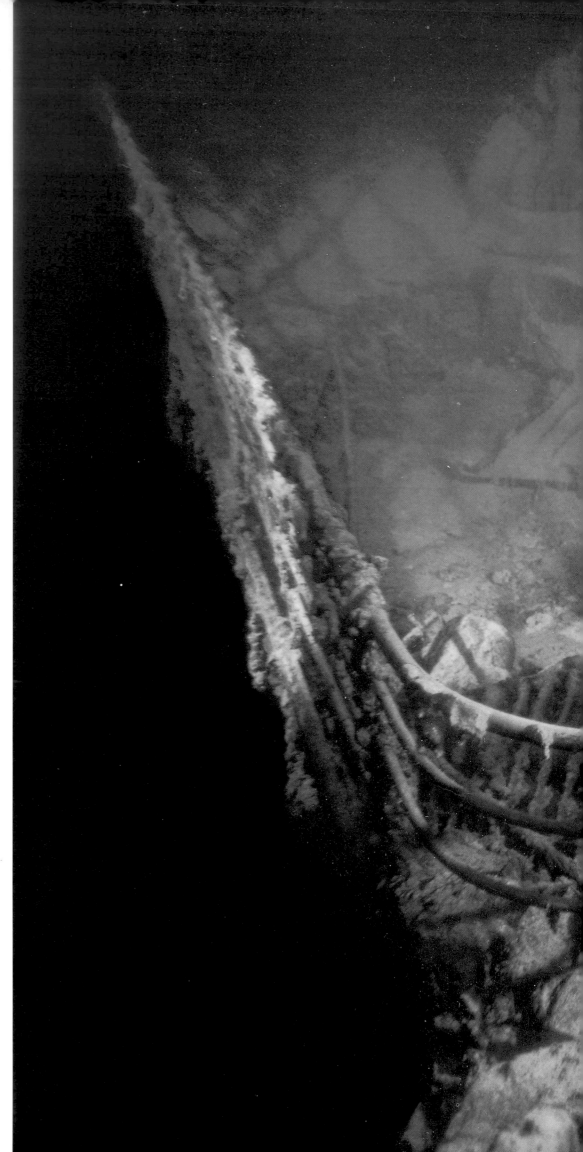

TITANIC

The *Titanic*'s bows and spare anchor are revealed in the blackness of the depths in the film *Titanica*.

TITANIC

ABOVE: The starboard Boat Deck with the expansion joint forced apart when *Titanic* hit the sea bed as seen in *Titanica*.

RIGHT: The little robot camera *Robin* descended within the ship and here we can see one of the *Titanic*'s light fittings.

ABOVE: This watch belonged to Mr. Brown, Edith Haisman's father. After it was restored it was presented to Mrs. Haisman.

ABOVE LEFT: A ceramic toothpaste lid lying on the sea bed.

LEFT: One of the crankshaft rings from *Titanic*'s engines is brought to the surface.

TITANIC

ABOVE: The recovery of a
lifeboat davit that was
lying on the sea bed.

RIGHT: A set of taps sal-
vaged from the wreck.

BELOW LEFT: A plate from the First Class section raised from the wreck site.

LEFT: A spittoon raised from the debris field in June 1993.

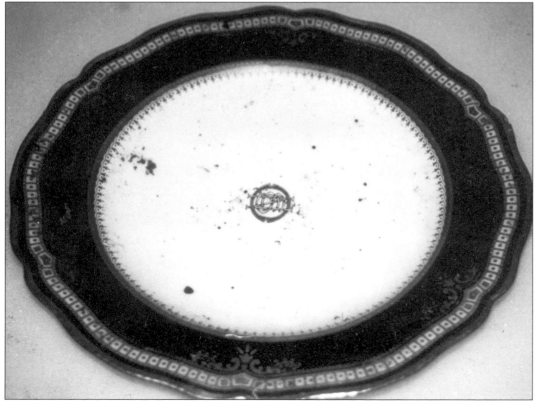

ABOVE: A metre-long rat-tail fish swims through the debris field above wine bottles and chamber pots.

RIGHT: Another view of the Titanic's bows.

BELOW RIGHT: Casseroles from the dining room.

LEFT: A cherub from *Titanic*'s aft first class staircase undergoes conservation treatment

BELOW LEFT: Conservator at work on a leather Gladstone bag

OVERLEAF: A model of the bow section which lies nearly 2½ miles down on the bottom of the Atlantic.